Microsoft® Office Outlook® 2013: Part 1 (Desktop/ Office 365™)

Microsoft® Office Outlook® 2013: Part 1 (Desktop/Office 365™)

Part Number: 091043
Course Edition: 3.0

Acknowledgements

PROJECT TEAM

Author	Media Designer	Content Editor
Lindsay Bachman	Alex Tong	Angie French

Notices

DISCLAIMER

TRADEMARK NOTICES

Microsoft® Office Outlook® 2013: Part 1 (Desktop/Office 365™)

About This Course

Email has become one of the most widely used methods of communication, whether for personal or business communications. In most organizations, large or small, email is the preferred form of communicating information amongst employees. As email grows in popularity and use, most organizations have found the need to implement a corporate mail management system such as Microsoft® Office Outlook® to handle the emails and meeting invitations sent among employees.

In this course, you will explore the Outlook interface and when you are familiar with it, you will use Outlook to manage all aspects of email communications; use the Outlook calendar to manage appointments and meetings; use Outlook's **People** workspace to manage your contact information; create Tasks and Notes for yourself in Outlook; and customize the Outlook interface to serve your own personal needs.

This course is the first in a series of two Microsoft® Office Outlook® 2013 courses. It will provide you with the basic skills you need to start using Outlook 2013 to manage your email communications, calendar events, contact information, tasks, and notes. You can also use this course to prepare for the Microsoft Office Specialist (MOS) Certification exams for Microsoft Outlook 2013.

Course Description

Target Student

This course is intended for people who have a basic understanding of Microsoft® Windows® and want or need to know how to use Outlook as an email client to manage their email communications, calendar events, contact information, and other communication tasks.

Course Prerequisites

To ensure success, students should be familiar with using personal computers, and should have experience using a keyboard and mouse. Students should be comfortable in the Windows® 8 environment, and be able to use Windows 8 to manage information on their computers. Specific tasks the students should be able to perform include: launching and closing applications, navigating basic file structures, and managing files and folders. Before starting this course, students should have completed one or more of the following courses or possess the equivalent knowledge:

- *Using Microsoft® Windows® 8*
- *Microsoft® Windows® 8: Transition from Windows® 7*

Course Objectives

In this course, you will become familiar with the Outlook 2013 interface, and then use Outlook to manage your email communications, including composing, reading, and responding to emails; schedule appointments and meetings; manage contact information; schedule tasks and create notes; and customize the Outlook environment to suit your personal preferences.

You will:

- Perform basic functions in the Outlook 2013 interface.
- Compose email messages.
- Read and respond to email messages.
- Manage email messages.
- Manage your calendar.
- Manage your contacts.
- Work with tasks and notes.
- Customize the Outlook environment.

The CHOICE Home Screen

Logon and access information for your CHOICE environment will be provided with your class experience. The CHOICE platform is your entry point to the CHOICE learning experience, of which this course manual is only one part.

On the CHOICE Home screen, you can access the CHOICE Course screens for your specific courses. Visit the CHOICE Course screen both during and after class to make use of the world of support and instructional resources that make up the CHOICE experience.

Each CHOICE Course screen will give you access to the following resources:

- **Classroom**: A link to your training provider's classroom environment.
- **eBook**: An interactive electronic version of the printed book for your course.
- **Files**: Any course files available to download.
- **Checklists**: Step-by-step procedures and general guidelines you can use as a reference during and after class.
- **LearnTOs**: Brief animated videos that enhance and extend the classroom learning experience.
- **Assessment**: A course assessment for your self-assessment of the course content.
- Social media resources that enable you to collaborate with others in the learning community using professional communications sites such as LinkedIn or microblogging tools such as Twitter.

Depending on the nature of your course and the components chosen by your learning provider, the CHOICE Course screen may also include access to elements such as:

- LogicalLABS, a virtual technical environment for your course.
- Various partner resources related to the courseware.
- Related certifications or credentials.
- A link to your training provider's website.
- Notices from the CHOICE administrator.
- Newsletters and other communications from your learning provider.
- Mentoring services.

Visit your CHOICE Home screen often to connect, communicate, and extend your learning experience!

How to Use This Book

As You Learn

This book is divided into lessons and topics, covering a subject or a set of related subjects. In most cases, lessons are arranged in order of increasing proficiency.

The results-oriented topics include relevant and supporting information you need to master the content. Each topic has various types of activities designed to enable you to solidify your understanding of the informational material presented in the course. Information is provided for reference and reflection to facilitate understanding and practice.

Data files for various activities as well as other supporting files for the course are available by download from the CHOICE Course screen. In addition to sample data for the course exercises, the course files may contain media components to enhance your learning and additional reference materials for use both during and after the course.

Checklists of procedures and guidelines can be used during class and as after-class references when you're back on the job and need to refresh your understanding.

At the back of the book, you will find a glossary of the definitions of the terms and concepts used throughout the course. You will also find an index to assist in locating information within the instructional components of the book.

As You Review

Any method of instruction is only as effective as the time and effort you, the student, are willing to invest in it. In addition, some of the information that you learn in class may not be important to you immediately, but it may become important later. For this reason, we encourage you to spend some time reviewing the content of the course after your time in the classroom.

As a Reference

The organization and layout of this book make it an easy-to-use resource for future reference. Taking advantage of the glossary, index, and table of contents, you can use this book as a first source of definitions, background information, and summaries.

Course Icons

Watch throughout the material for the following visual cues.

Icon	Description
	A **Note** provides additional information, guidance, or hints about a topic or task.
	A **Caution** note makes you aware of places where you need to be particularly careful with your actions, settings, or decisions so that you can be sure to get the desired results of an activity or task.
	LearnTO notes show you where an associated LearnTO is particularly relevant to the content. Access LearnTOs from your CHOICE Course screen.
	Checklists provide job aids you can use after class as a reference to perform skills back on the job. Access checklists from your CHOICE Course screen.
	Social notes remind you to check your CHOICE Course screen for opportunities to interact with the CHOICE community using social media.

1 | Getting Started With Outlook 2013

Lesson Time: 1 hour

Lesson Objectives

In this lesson, you will:

- Navigate the Outlook interface.

- Perform basic email functions.

- Use Outlook Help.

Lesson Introduction

Chances are, if you work for an organization that's even moderately sized, you are using an mail management system such as Microsoft® Office Outlook® to handle your communications. You need to be familiar with the Outlook interface and comfortable using the application to perform the required basic email functions. In this lesson, you will start using Outlook.

In order to use the Outlook 2013, you will need to know how to navigate the interface and know how to perform basic email functions like creating and sending an email, reading and responding to an email, and even printing or deleting an email. And, if you find yourself needing some assistance while in the interface, you need to know how to use the Outlook Help tool to provide you with the necessary information. Knowing the interface and how to use its components will enable you to perform any of the basic email functions that will be required of you in an email-friendly work environment.

TOPIC A

Navigate the Outlook Interface

Before you can even begin to use Outlook 2013, you need to become familiar with the interface and the components of the application. In this topic, you will navigate the Outlook interface.

Knowing how to navigate within the interface and how all of the components of the application function will help you become familiar with the ins and outs of the Outlook 2013 environment before you even begin working with the application. When you are comfortable and familiar with the tool and how it works, you will be able to more quickly and easily use the application to begin sending and receiving emails.

Email

Email, or electronic mail, refers to electronic mail messages that can be delivered and exchanged between one sender and one or more recipients. Email messages are nearly immediate in nature; depending on the size of the email and barring any technical errors in delivery, an email message is received immediately upon being sent. It is then dependent on the recipients to read and respond to the message as needed or as they see fit. Email is one of the most common methods of communication being used for instances when multiple people need to be involved in a single conversation and a response is needed in a timely manner. For this reason, email is growing quickly in both the business world and in personal communications as the preferred method of communication.

Email Clients

In order to send and receive email messages, an email client is needed. The email client is an application that is used to access, display, and interact with the electronic messages.

Email Addresses

Email messages are sent from one email address to another. An email address is a string of information that specifies a person and place to send the message to. An email address is made up of three parts:

- The local part, which is a unique user name made up of alphabetic and numeric characters, and possibly special characters like an underscore.
- The @ symbol immediately after the local part.
- The domain part, which is a hostname and a standard extension such as .com or .net.

The local part   The domain part

Dietrich.Brown@develetech.example

Figure 1–1: An email address.

Microsoft Outlook 2013

Microsoft Outlook 2013 is the email client that is provided with the Microsoft Office 2013 suite of products. Using Outlook 2013, users can access and interact with email messages and the information included with those messages, including reading and responding to emails, saving and sending messages to contacts, and keeping track of appointments and meetings using the calendar.

> **Note: Outlook on the Web**
> Through your Office 365™ subscription, you have access to the Outlook on the Web app. Throughout this course, you will see notes that identify any significant differences between the desktop application and the online app.

Office Online Apps

When you purchase an Office 365 subscription, you also have access to the Office Online apps which include Microsoft® Excel®, Microsoft® Word, Microsoft® PowerPoint®, Outlook, and a variety of other apps. You can use any web browser to access Office 365 by navigating to **login.microsoftonline.com** and signing in with your Office 365 user account and password. These online apps are scaled-down versions of the Office 2013 desktop applications and provide basic features and some of the same functionality that exists in the desktop applications. The advantage of using the Office Online apps is the ability to access, edit, share, and store your online files across a variety of devices.

Items and Folders

There are two basic elements in Outlook that you will interact with: items and folders.

Items in Outlook contain the information that you are viewing or working with. Items include email messages, calendar entries, contact information, tasks, and notes.

Folders are the organizational containers in which items in Outlook are stored. Folders are most often used to organize your email messages. Some folders are included as defaults with an Outlook installation to help manage your mail, including the **Inbox, Drafts, Sent Items, Deleted Items, Outbox, RSS Feeds,** and **Search Folders** folders. New folders can be created to group items that are related to one another and help you easily find and manage your Outlook items.

Components of the Outlook Interface

There are a number of standard components that make up the Outlook 2013 interface.

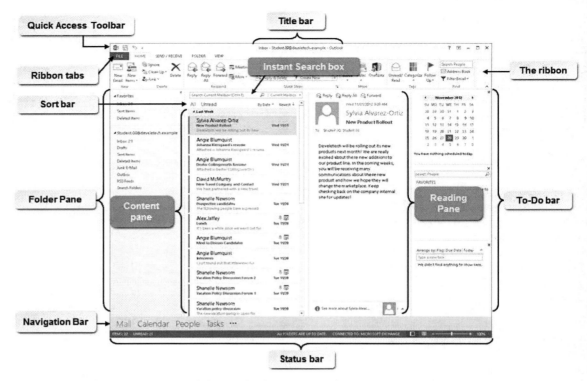

Figure 1-2: The components of the Outlook 2013 interface.

Component	Description
Title bar	The title bar is located at the very top of the window, and displays the title of the folder where you are currently located, the name of the email account you are viewing, and the name of the application (Microsoft Outlook).
Quick Access Toolbar	The **Quick Access Toolbar** is located at the top of the window, to the left of the title bar. It displays a number of commands that are commonly used within the interface, providing easy access to these tools.
The ribbon	The ribbon is located below the title bar in the window. It displays and provides access to all of the commands needed to perform actions within the Outlook interface.
Ribbon tabs	The ribbon tabs are located along the top of the window on the ribbon, below the title bar and the **Quick Access Toolbar**. Each tab contains command buttons that perform specific Outlook functions.
Folder pane	The **Folder** pane is located at the left side of the Outlook window. It displays and provides access to all of the folders available in the Outlook environment for the email account you are viewing, including the Inbox for the account. You can customize what folders appear and in what order they appear.
Content pane	The **Content** pane is located in the middle of the Outlook window, to the immediate right of the **Folder** pane. It displays all of the individual items within the specific folder where you are located. For instance, when in the **Inbox** folder in the **Navigation** pane, the **Content** pane displays the message list of all of the messages currently in the Inbox. When in the Calendar, the **Content** pane displays the meetings you have scheduled during a specific time frame.

Component	Description
Sort bar	The sort bar is located above the item list in the **Content** pane. It displays the titles of all the columns that are currently being shown for your Outlook items, and can be used to arrange or sort how the items are displayed in the pane (sorted by subject, sorted by size, and more).
Instant Search box	The **Instant Search** box is located at the top of the **Content** pane, above the sort bar. It is used to enter a term or keyword, and searches your Outlook items for instances of that term. It then displays the resulting items that contain that term somewhere in their contents.
Reading pane	The **Reading** pane is located at the right side of the Outlook window, to the immediate right of the **Content** pane. It displays the contents of the Outlook item you have currently selected, such as the contents of an email message you have selected in the **Content** pane for the Inbox. It provides a preview of the contents of the item before it is opened in a separate Outlook window.
To-Do Bar	By default, the **To-Do Bar** does not display in Outlook 2013. However, if desired, you can enable the **To-Do Bar** to display a high-level view of the Calendar, People, and Tasks workspaces. If enabled, the **To-Do Bar** displays at the far right side of the Outlook window, to the right of the **Reading** pane.
Navigation bar	The **Navigation** bar is located below the **Folder, Content,** and **Reading** panes. It displays launch buttons for the other Outlook workspaces like the Calendar, People, and Tasks workspaces.
Status bar	The status bar is located at the very bottom of the Outlook window. It displays information related to the folder you are currently in, such as the number of items in the folder, if the folder is up-to-date or is currently sending or receiving information, and more.

 Note: More information about customizing the Outlook environment to suit your own personal preferences is presented later on in this course.

ScreenTips

When you hover your mouse pointer over a command icon or button in the Outlook window, a small window with descriptive text will appear. These text windows are called ScreenTips, and they provide information about what action the command or button performs.

 Note: Outlook on the Web

The online app user interface is noticeably scaled down from the desktop application. The **Quick Access Toolbar** is not available in the online app, and instead of the **Navigation bar,** you use the **App Launcher** icon ▦ to access the tiles for **Calendar, People,** and **Tasks.**

Components of the Ribbon

The ribbon is made up of two parts: the tabs and the command groups that make up each tab. Each tab has an organizational title that references the specific functions that the command groups within that tab provide. Each command group also has an organizational title, with the specific commands within each group associated with a specific task in the Outlook environment.

Figure 1-3: The components of the Ribbon in Outlook 2013.

There are five default ribbon tabs. Each provides access to the commands within the tab that perform an action.

Ribbon Tab	Description
FILE	The **FILE** tab provides access to various commands related to both the Outlook environment in general, or the active Outlook item you are working with. Item-specific tasks in the **FILE** tab include **Save As, Save Attachments,** and **Print.** For more general environment-related tasks, the **FILE** tab provides access to the **Info, Open & Export, Help, Office Account,** and **Options** commands.
HOME	The commands displayed on the **HOME** tab will vary depending on whether you are working in the Outlook window or within an active item. Each Outlook item will display different command groups that are specific to the actions needed for that item. The **HOME** tab may display a different title for some types of items when the item is active in a new window: **MESSAGE** for emails, **APPOINTMENT** or **MEETING** for calendar entries, **CONTACT** for contact entries, and **TASK** for tasks.
SEND/RECEIVE	The **SEND/RECEIVE** tab displays commands specific to synchronizing, sending, and receiving data for Outlook items. It also includes commands to download items and work offline.
FOLDER	The **FOLDER** tab displays commands used to create, move, delete, and generally manage any folders in the Outlook environment. There are also commands available for managing folder contents, organizing folders, and setting folder properties.
VIEW	The **VIEW** tab displays commands used for setting or adjusting the layout of the Outlook window and how items are displayed within the window.

Dialog Box Launchers

Some command groups on the ribbon will have a small downward-arrow button located at the bottom-right corner of the command group box. The button is called a *Dialog Box Launcher,* and when selected, opens a dialog box with additional features available for that command group.

Note: Outlook on the Web

Unlike the desktop app, the online app has a **command bar** instead of the familiar ribbon. This is a scaled-down version of the full desktop application's ribbon and the commands are specific to the selected window component. For example, if a message is selected, the **Delete, Archive, Move to** and **Categories** commands appear. If a folder is selected, then you will see the **Empty folder** command.

Note: The ribbon is a feature of all products in the Office 2013 suite. For more information, check out the LearnTO **Navigate the Office 2013 Ribbon** presentation from the **LearnTO** tile on the CHOICE Course screen.

The Backstage View

The **Backstage View** is a feature provided in all Microsoft Office products. The **Backstage View** is a single location where you manage features and properties of either the Outlook application or of specific active items. You access the **Backstage View** by selecting the **File** tab in the window.

When launched for the application, the **Backstage View** displays the **Account Information** page on the **Info** tab by default. From the **Account Information** page, you can manage your Outlook account, including modifying account settings, enabling automatic replies, or using the mailbox cleanup tools.

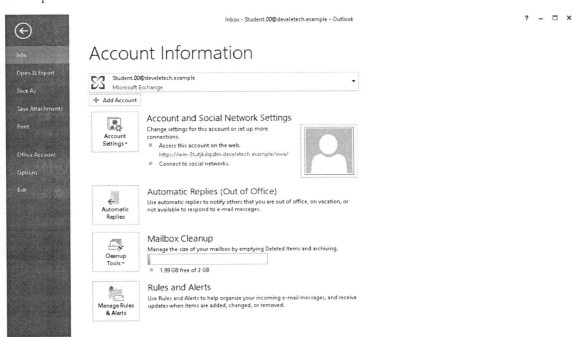

Figure 1-4: The Backstage View in Outlook 2013.

From the **Backstage View** for the application, you can also open other calendars or data files, import or export files, print items, manage your Office Account, access the **Outlook Options** dialog box, or exit the application.

When launched for an Outlook item, the **Backstage View** displays information, options, and properties specific to the item type. From the **Backstage View** for an item, you can view the properties for the item, manage the location of the item, and for mail messages, manage permissions and other settings.

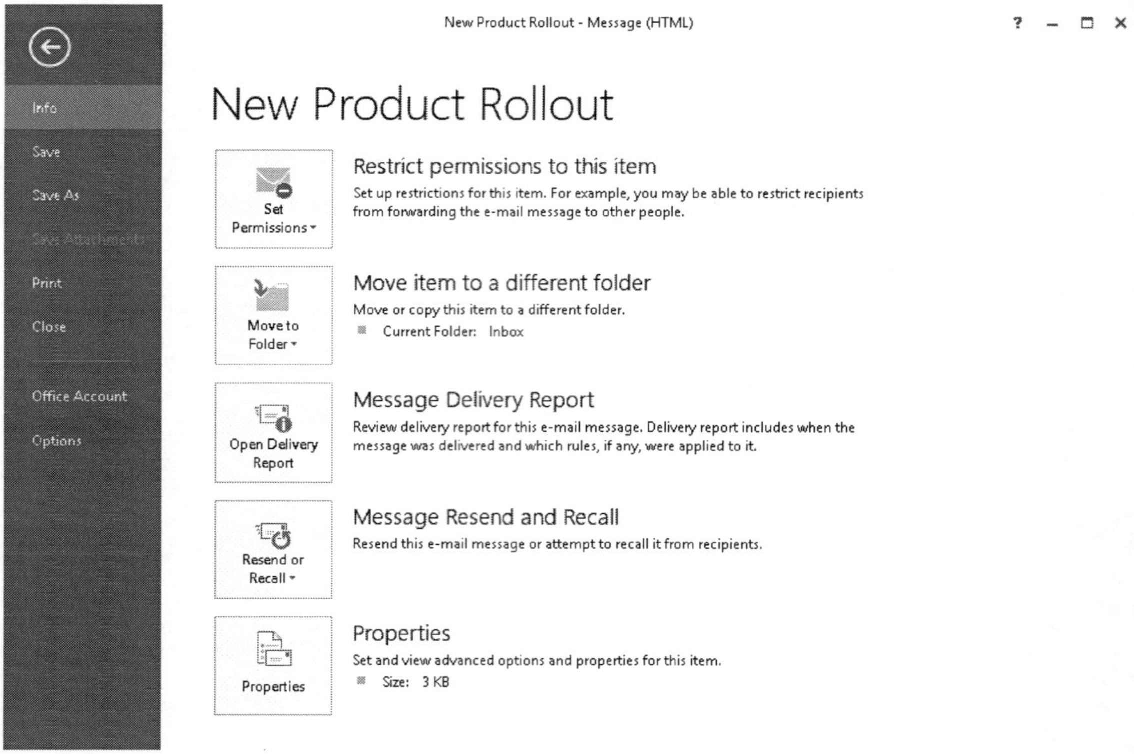
New Product Rollout - Message (HTML)
Info
Save
Save As
Save Attachments
Print
Close
Office Account
Options
New Product Rollout
Set Permissions
Restrict permissions to this item
Set up restrictions for this item. For example, you may be able to restrict recipients from forwarding the e-mail message to other people.
Move to Folder
Move item to a different folder
Move or copy this item to a different folder.
Current Folder: Inbox
Open Delivery Report
Message Delivery Report
Review delivery report for this e-mail message. Delivery report includes when the message was delivered and which rules, if any, were applied to it.
Resend or Recall
Message Resend and Recall
Resend this e-mail message or attempt to recall it from recipients.
Properties
Properties
Set and view advanced options and properties for this item.
Size: 3 KB

Figure 1-5: The Backstage View for an email message in Outlook.

From the **Backstage View** for the item, you can also save items or attachments, print the active item, close the active item, manage your Office Account, or access the **Outlook Options** dialog box.

Note: Outlook on the Web

Instead of a **Backstage** view, the buttons at the far right end of the command bar can be used to control Outlook settings and access account information. You can access and configure notifications, Outlook options, help, and your account settings.

The Mail Workspace

The **Mail** workspace is the default view in the Outlook environment. The **Mail** workspace is where you will work with all of the email messages you send and receive.

Email messages and some other Outlook items are stored in the various mail folders in Outlook. These folders appear in the **Folder** pane of the Outlook window.

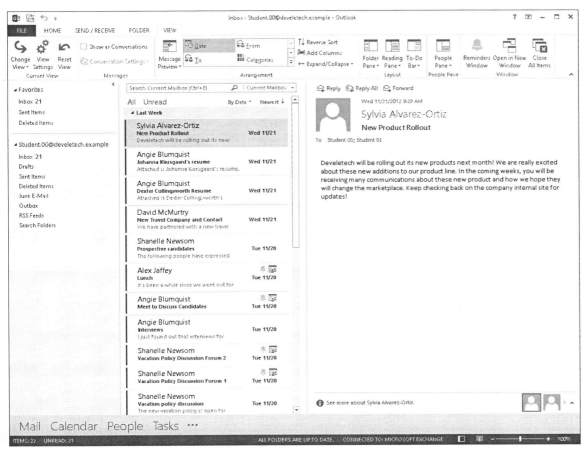

Figure 1-6: The Mail workspace in Outlook 2013.

Note: Outlook on the Web

In the online app, your mail is displayed in a scaled-down version of the desktop application **Mail** view that is shown here. The **Folder** pane, message list, search field, and **Reading** pane function in a similar manner. Instead of the ribbon running horizontally across the top of the window, you will see the Office 365 header with the **App Launcher** icon at the far left and icons to access notifications, application settings, and help at the far right end.

Mail Folders

The default folders in Outlook include the following.

Mail Folder	Description
Inbox	By default, the **Inbox** folder is opened when Outlook is launched. The Inbox displays all of the email messages and meeting invitations or responses that have been received by the user. The items in the Inbox are displayed in the **View** pane in the Outlook interface, and the contents of the selected or active item is displayed in the **Reading** pane.
Drafts	The **Drafts** folder stores copies of email messages that are in progress of being composed, or have been composed and not sent. You can access these unfinished messages in the folder at a later time to be completed and sent.

Mail Folder	Description
Sent Items	The **Sent Items** folder stores copies of Outlook items that you have previously sent, including email messages, meeting invites, and meeting responses. By default, items that you send are stored in the **Sent Items** folder, though you can configure these items to be saved to an alternative location.
Deleted Items	The **Deleted Items** folder stores all of the Outlook items that you have deleted from other folders.
Junk E-mail	The **Junk E-Mail** folder stores any email messages from unknown or untrusted senders that appear to be spam or junk mail.
Outbox	The **Outbox** folder temporarily stores email messages that have been sent while they are in the process of being delivered to the recipient.
RSS Feeds	The **RSS Feeds** folder is used to access the items from website you have subscribed to using an Real Simple Syndication (RSS) feed.
Search Folders	The **Search Folders** folder is used to access any search folders you have created in Outlook to search for specific keywords or phrases.

Read and Unread Messages

Outlook visually differentiates the messages in your message list that are read or unread. If a message is unread, the subject line displays in blue, bold font and a vertical blue bar appears next to the message in the message list. Once the message has been selected and viewed, even in the **Reading** pane, the blue bar and blue, bold font in the subject line no longer appear to show that the message has been read.

> **Note:** When the **Reading** pane displays at the right of the Outlook window, as it does by default, both the blue bar and the blue, bold font display to denote an unread message. If you choose to display the **Reading** pane at the bottom of the Outlook window, the blue bar is not displayed; only blue, bold font displays to denote an unread message.

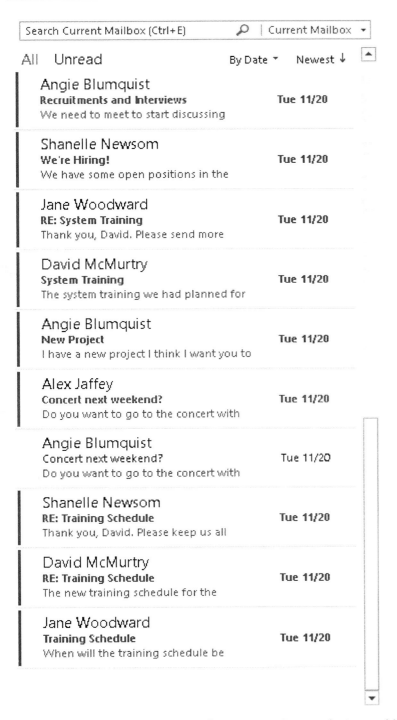

Figure 1–7: Unread messages in the message list are designated by blue, bold font in the subject line and a vertical blue bar next to the message.

Message Icons

One or more message icons may appear in association with the messages in the Inbox. Each icon conveys information about that particular Outlook message that may help you react to and manage your email messages appropriately. There are a few icons that are commonly seen in relation to emails.

Icon	Description
Replied To: The email message was replied to.
Forwarded: The email message has been forwarded.
High Importance: The email message contains important and potentially time-sensitive information, and should be read or/and replied to as soon as possible.
Attachment: The email contains an attached document.
Flagged for Follow-Up: This email has been flagged by you for follow-up. The **Flag** icon serves as a reminder that you need to follow-up with an action or a response to this email by a certain date or time.

 Note: You won't necessarily see all of the available icons in your Inbox; some icons don't apply to your items unless you have activated settings or options within the environment.

 Note: There are other icons that you may see in your Inbox regarding other Outlook tools, such as the **Calendar** or **Tasks**. More information is available about those icons where those tools are covered in this course.

The Calendar Workspace

The **Calendar** workspace is used for scheduling and managing any personal or professional events that you are participating in.

The **Calendar** workspace contains two main components: the **Folder** pane and the calendar grid. The **Folder** pane displays the calendar for the current month and the following month, and provides navigation through the months of the year. When a date is selected on the calendar, it displays in the calendar grid. The default view for the calendar grid is the **Month** view, which displays the entire month, with the current date highlighted. Any appointments or meetings scheduled throughout the month will display on the appropriate day in the calendar.

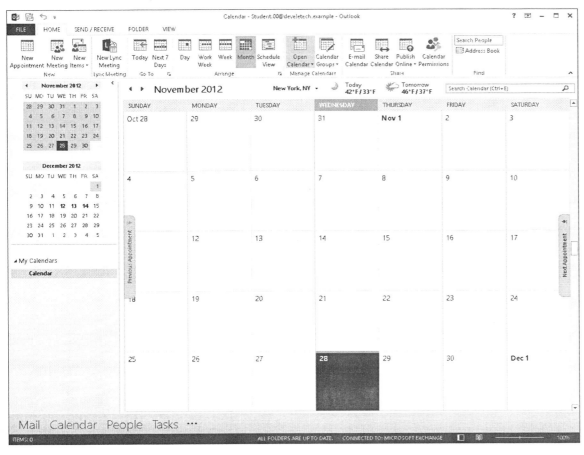

Figure 1-8: The Calendar workspace in Outlook 2013.

Note: You can customize how the **Calendar** workspace appears. More information about customizing the Outlook environment to suit your own personal preferences is presented later in this course.

Note: Outlook on the Web

To navigate to your calendar, you can select the **App Launcher** icon and then select the **Calendar** tile. You can use this same technique to open the **People** and **Tasks** workspaces as well.

The People Workspace

The **People** workspace is used to create and manage your own personal address book of people with whom you communicate on a regular basis.

The **People** workspace contains three main components: the **Folder** pane where your folders are displayed, the **Content** pane where your contacts are displayed, and the **Reading** pane where the selected contact's information is displayed. Your contacts are displayed by default in the **Content** pane using a business card format, which displays contact details for each person. From the **People** workspace, you can edit existing contacts, create new contacts, create new contact groups, and quickly perform an action such as email a selected contact.

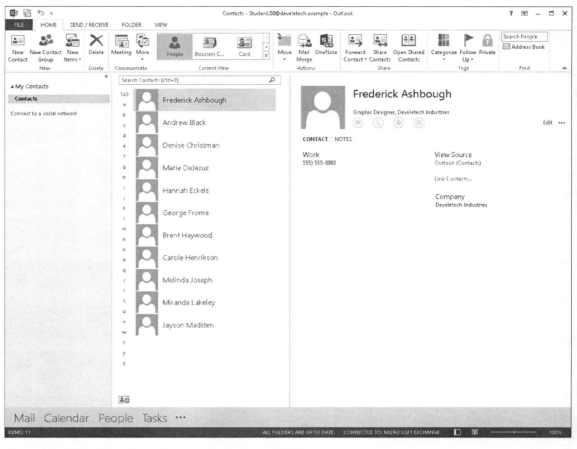

Figure 1-9: The People workspace in Outlook 2013.

 Note: You can customize how the **People** workspace appears. More information about customizing the Outlook environment to suit your own personal preferences is presented later in this course.

Additional Outlook Tools

There are a number of additional tools available in Outlook 2013.

 Note: Outlook on the Web

In the online app, each of the workspaces discussed here are accessed in different ways. You can open your Tasks by selecting the **App Launcher** and then selecting the **Tasks** tile. Notes are stored in the **Notes** folder in Mail. And, the **Journal** feature is unavailable in the online app.

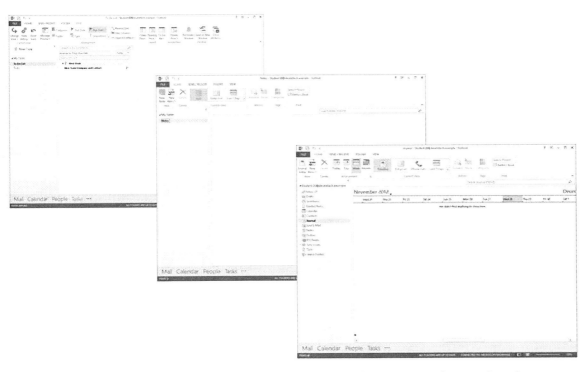

Figure 1-10: The additional tools in Outlook include the Tasks, Notes, and Journal workspaces.

- **Tasks:** Found in the **Tasks** workspace, Tasks allow you to create assignments to complete a specific action or contribute to a piece of work within a certain amount of time. You can assign tasks to yourself or other people. Tasks assigned to you will also appear in your **To-Do** list.
- **Notes:** Found in the **Notes** workspace, Notes allow you to capture important information that you don't want to forget or lose track of and save within your Outlook environment. When you visit the **Notes** section, you can view all of the notes you have left for yourself. Notes can be assigned to categories and distinguished by different category colors for easy identification.
- **Journal:** The journal, found in the **Journal** workspace, allows you to track and record actions for Outlook items, including email messages, meeting invites and responses, tasks, or phone conversations, that are associated with a specific contact. Activities, actions, and completed items are displayed in a timeline view within the **Journal** tool.

Note: In Outlook 2013, the **Journal** feature is being phased out as a top-level workspace. The **Journal** tool is still available within Outlook, but it is no longer accessed using the **Navigation** bar. To access the **Journal,** you first have to access **Folders** under **More Options** for the **Navigation** bar. The **Journal** will then appear as a folder in the **Folder** pane, which you can then select to launch the **Journal** workspace.

Peeks

The Peeks feature in Outlook allows you to see a preview of your other workspaces without having to leave the workspace in which you are currently working. For instance, if you are in the **Mail** workspace, but want to get a quick idea of any upcoming calendar events, you can hover over the **Calendar** button in the Quick Launch bar and Outlook will display a peek of your calendar information.

The Peeks feature will display a preview for your Mail, Calendar, People, and Tasks workspaces.

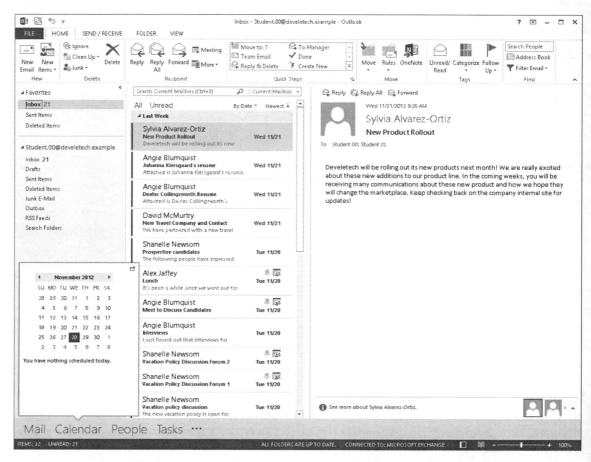

Figure 1-11: The Peeks feature shows a preview of the Calendar workspace from the Mail workspace.

Note: Outlook on the Web

Because the **Navigation bar** is not a component of the online app, this feature is also not available. To switch between your mail, calendar, contacts, and tasks, you will use the **App Launcher** icon and the associated tiles.

ACTIVITY 1-1
Exploring the Outlook 2013 Interface

Scenario

You work for Develetech Industries, a mid-sized company that designs and manufactures home electronics. Develetech has just rolled out Outlook 2013 as its new email application. Before you begin using Outlook to communicate via email, it is a good idea to familiarize yourself with the Outlook interface and its components.

 Note: Activities may vary slightly if the software vendor has issued digital updates. Your instructor will notify you of any changes.

1. Launch Outlook 2013.
   a) On the **Start** screen, right-click anywhere on the screen and at the bottom of the screen select **All apps**.
   b) Under **Microsoft Office 2013**, select **Outlook 2013**.

    Note: If the computer is set up for multiple users, you may need to select your profile when Outlook starts. In the **Choose Profile** dialog box, select your profile from the **Profile Name** drop-down list and select **OK**.

2. Explore the **Mail** workspace.

    Note: By default, Outlook opens in the Inbox, in the **Mail** workspace.

   a) Select a message in the message list in the **Content** pane.
   b) View the message body in the **Reading** pane.
   c) Select the other default folders in the **Folder** pane to view their contents. (Except for the Inbox, the folders are empty at this point.)
   d) On the **HOME** tab, view the tab's command groups and commands.
   e) Select the other ribbon tabs in the **Mail** workspace and view the commands that display on the ribbon for each.

3. Explore the **Quick Access Toolbar**.
   a) View the icons currently displaying in the **Quick Access Toolbar** at the top-left of the screen, to the left of the title bar.
   b) On the **Quick Access Toolbar**, select the **Customize Quick Access Toolbar** drop-down arrow ▼ to view the customization options in the drop-down list.
   c) Select the drop-down arrow again to close the list.

4. View the available components of the **To-Do Bar** and how they appear if enabled.
   a) Select the **VIEW** tab and select the **To-Do Bar** command to view the available components of the **To-Do Bar**.
   b) Select one of the available components and view how it appears in the **To-Do Bar**.
   c) Select the close button at the top of the **To-Do Bar** to close the component and disable the **To-Do Bar**.

5. Explore the **Calendar** workspace.

a) In the **Navigation** bar, select **Calendar**.
b) View the calendar that opens in the calendar grid.
c) In the **Folder** pane, select a different day from the calendar, and view how the date in the calendar grid changes.
d) Select the **VIEW** tab to view the tab's command groups and commands.
e) In the **Arrangement** command group, select the commands for the various calendar views to display a different view in the calendar grid.
f) Select the **Month** view in the **Arrangement** to return the view to the default option.
g) Select the other ribbon tabs in the **Calendar** workspace and view the commands that display on the ribbon for each.

 Note: Notice how the command groups and commands are different on the ribbon tabs for the **Calendar** than those that appeared in the **Mail** workspace.

6. Explore the **People** workspace.
   a) In the **Navigation** bar, select **People**.
   b) View the contacts that appear in the **Content** pane.
   c) View the commands that appear on the **HOME** tab in the ribbon.
   d) Select the other ribbon tabs and view the commands that display on the ribbon for each.

 Note: Notice how the command groups and commands are different on the ribbon tabs for **People** than those that appeared in the other workspaces you have already explored.

7. Explore the **Tasks** workspace.
   a) In the **Navigation** bar, select **Tasks**.
   b) View the **To-Do** list in the **Content** pane that appears automatically. (No items are listed at this point.)
   c) In the **Folder** pane, select **Tasks** and view the tasks list in the **Content** pane. (No items are listed at this point.)
   d) View the commands that appear on the **HOME** tab in the ribbon.
   e) Select the other ribbon tabs and view the commands that display on the ribbon for each.

 Note: Notice how the command groups and commands are different on the ribbon tabs for **Tasks** than those that appeared in the other workspaces you have already explored.

8. Explore the **Backstage View**.
   a) Select the **FILE** tab.
   b) View the account information that displays on the default **Info** page.
   c) Select **Open & Export** and view the options.
   d) Select **Print** and view the options.
   e) Select **Office Account** and view the **Account** information.
   f) Select **Options** to open the **Outlook Options** dialog box.
   g) Select **Cancel** to close the **Outlook Options** dialog box.

9. In the **Navigation** bar, select **Mail** to return to the **Mail** workspace.

TOPIC B

Perform Basic Email Functions

Once you are familiar with the Outlook 2013 environment, you are ready to start using the application to communicate with others. In this topic, you will perform basic Outlook email functions.

Outlook is used to send and receive communications in the form of emails. When you know how to perform all the basic Outlook email functions—creating and sending new emails, reading and responding to an email, even printing and deleting an email—you are ready to start using Outlook as a communication tool.

The Message Form

The message form is the window that is launched in Outlook when you create a new email or respond to an email. In the message form, you will:

- Add your primary recipients in the **To** field and any secondary recipients to be copied on the message in the **Cc** field.
- Add the subject matter or purpose of the email in the **Subject** field.
- Add the content of your message in the message body.

 Note: The **Bcc** and **From** fields do not automatically display in the message form window, but can be added to the message form optionally.

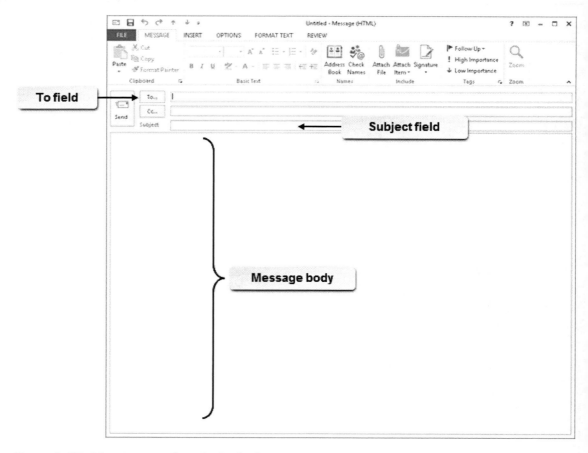

Figure 1-12: The message form in Outlook.

Cc vs. Bcc

Recipients included in the **Cc** (carbon copy) field will receive a copy of the email message, and will be visible as a recipient of the message. Recipients included in the **Bcc** (blind carbon copy) field will receive a copy of the message, but they are invisible to the other recipients as being included on the message.

> **Note: Outlook on the Web**
>
> When you select the **New** button, a new message appears on the right side of the window instead of in a separate own window. Unlike the message form in the desktop application, the available commands and options are slightly scaled back.

Message Form Tabs

The ribbon on the message form displays tabs and command groups that provide specific options and features to use when composing an email.

Figure 1-13: The Ribbon and tabs on a Message form.

Message Form Tab	Description
FILE	The **FILE** tab opens the **Backstage View** for that email message. The **Info** section of the **Backstage View** for the message provides a location where you can set permissions and advanced properties for the message if needed or desired.
MESSAGE	The **MESSAGE** tab provides actions and options for basic email functions, such as using the clipboard, formatting text, attaching files or signatures, and tagging messages with follow-up options or priority levels.
INSERT	The **INSERT** tab provides actions and options for inserting various objects into your email message, such as including an Outlook item or inserting tables, illustrations, links, text, or symbols.
OPTIONS	The **OPTIONS** tab provides actions and options for enhancing your email with more advanced features, including adding a them, displaying hidden fields, setting permissions, using tracking features, and other options related to message delivery.
FORMAT TEXT	The **FORMAT TEXT** tab provides actions and options for common text formatting, such as using the clipboard, changing the text format, modifying the font and paragraph formatting, and applying styles.
REVIEW	The **REVIEW** tab provides actions and options for reviewing your email for proper grammar and usage before sending, such as using proofing tools like spellcheck or the thesaurus, and implementing language tools, if necessary.

 Access the Checklist tile on your CHOICE Course screen for reference information and job aids on How to Create and Send a New Email Message.

ACTIVITY 1-2
Creating and Sending an Email

Scenario

Develetech is growing and hiring many new employees. You have been asked to be part of a team working on a recruitment plan and the hiring process. You heard that your coworker, Alex Jaffey, will be on the team as well. You want to send a quick email to Alex to confirm his involvement in the project.

---

1. Create a new email to send to Alex Jaffey.

    a) On the **HOME** tab, select **New Email**.

    New
    Email

    b) In the **To** field, type *Alex.Jaffey@develetech.example*

    c) In the **Subject** , type *Recruitment team?*

    > **Note:** This is not a typing class. Unless otherwise noted or you are implicitly asked to type the text as indicated for the sake of the activity, you do not have to type the text verbatim, without mistakes, or you can type the text of your choice rather than the indicated text.

    d) In the message body, type *I heard that you might be working on the recruitment team for the graphic design hires?*

2. Send the email.

    a) Select **Send** to send the message to Alex.

Message Response Options

When you receive an email in Outlook and need to respond to the message, there are number of reply options that you can choose from when responding. Reply options are located in the **Respond** command group of the **MESSAGE** tab of the ribbon within an email message. These options include:

*   **Reply:** Creates a response email where the recipient is only the sender of the initial email.
*   **Reply All:** Creates a response email where the recipients include the sender and everyone who was a recipient of the initial email.
*   **Forward:** Creates a new email that contains the email message content from the initial email and can be sent to a new recipient, not including the sender of the initial email.

ACTIVITY 1-3
Reading and Responding to Emails

Scenario

Since you are part of the recruitment team, you have been included on a number of emails regarding the recruitment efforts and potential candidates. Your HR recruiter, Shanelle Newsom, has sent the team an email listing the potential candidates and requesting further candidates if you know of any. Your friend Asa is a multimedia designer and would be a good candidate for one of the open positions. You need to read and respond to Shanelle's email with this information.

You also want to forward the email from Shanelle about Develetech's hiring efforts to Asa. You will forward the email using the inline replies feature.

---

1. Read the email from Shanelle Newsom.
   a) In the message list in the **Content** pane, select the email from Shanelle Newsom with the subject line "Prospective Candidates."
   b) Read the message body in the **Reading** pane.

2. Reply to all recipients of the message with your response.
   a) On the **HOME** tab on the ribbon, in the **Respond** command group, select **Reply All**.

   Reply
   All

   b) In the message body, type *I have a friend who is a multimedia designer. He may be looking for a new position. I will send him the hiring information and ask him if he is interested.*
   c) Select **Send** to send the message to all recipients.

    Note: Because other students in the class will be using the **Reply All** option, and you were a recipient of the original email, you will receive the responses from your classmates. You will read these responses in Step 4.

3. Forward the We're Hiring! email from Shanelle to your friend Asa.
   a) In the message list, find and select the email from Shanelle Newsom with the subject line **We're Hiring!**
   b) In the **Reading** pane where the message content is displayed, select **Forward**.
   c) In the **To** field, type *Asa.Stern@example.edu*
   d) In the message body, type *Asa, thought you might be interested. If so, let me know ASAP.*
   e) Select **Send**.

4. Read one of the replies to the Prospective Candidates message that you just received.
   a) In the message list, find and select one of the responses you just received from your classmates with the subject line "RE: Prospective Candidates."

Print Options

Print Options, accessed via the **Backstage View,** allows you to specify the print settings for printing an Outlook item. **Print Options** opens the **Print** dialog box, where you can choose the settings for printing the document. In the dialog box, you can select the printer where you would like to print your document, specify the print style for the output (table or memo style), adjust the settings for the copies being made, specify the page range, and select other print options like printing attachments.

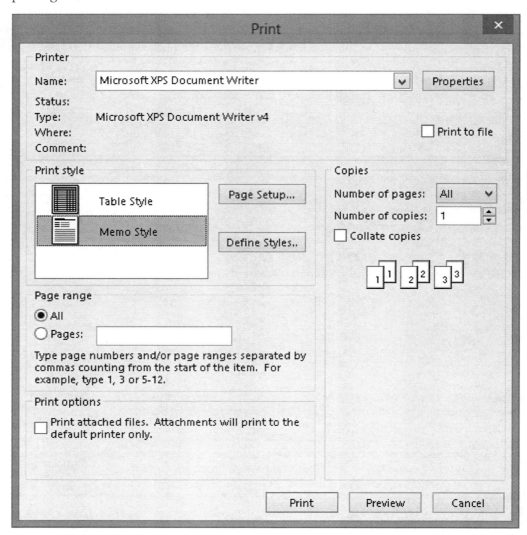

Figure 1-16: Selecting Print Options opens the Print dialog box.

Note: Outlook on the Web

When you print in Outlook on the Web, the required steps vary slightly from those used to print in Outlook 2013. You continue to have the ability to preview how the printout will look. From the command bar, select the **More commands** button and then select **Print**. The selected item, such as an email message, is first displayed in a separate window and then the **Print** window containing print settings appears.

Access the Checklist tile on your CHOICE Course screen for reference information and job aids on How to Print an Email Message.

ACTIVITY 1–4
Printing an Email Message

Before You Begin

If you do not have a physical printer available in the classroom where you can print documents during activities, a printer driver has been installed on your machine and paused to mimic printing.

Scenario

You want to print out the email that Shanelle sent with the list of potential candidates. You think that a friend of yours might know some of the people who have applied, and you want to get her professional opinion on them. You are meeting her for dinner later, and want to have the list of their names available to give her.

Print the email from Shanelle.

a) In the message list in the **Content** pane, select the email from Shanelle Newsom with the subject line "Prospective Candidates."

b) Select **FILE→Print**.

c) Select **Print**.

The Deleted Items Folder

Deleted messages and other Outlook items are moved to the **Deleted Items** folder. These items will remain in the **Deleted Items** folder until you manually and permanently delete each item or empty the folder. Items in the **Deleted Items** folder can be recovered to the Inbox or a folder you created until they have been permanently deleted.

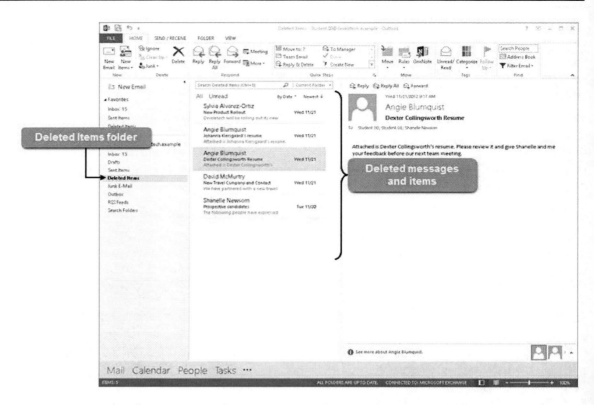

Figure 1-17: Deleted messages and items are moved to and stored in the Deleted Items folder.

 Access the Checklist tile on your CHOICE Course screen for reference information and job aids on **How to Delete an Email Message or Item.**

ACTIVITY 1-5
Deleting Email Messages

Scenario

You have a couple of old emails that you have read and no longer need to keep in your Inbox. You have the feeling that your **Deleted Items** folder is getting full, so after you delete some of these old messages, you also want to empty the folder to make more available space in your Inbox.

---

1. Delete unnecessary emails from your Inbox.
    a) In the message list, find and select the email from Angie Blumquist with the subject line "New project."
    b) On the **HOME** tab, select **Delete**.

    Delete

    c) In the message list, find and select the email from Alex Jaffey with the subject line "Concert next weekend?"
    d) Select **Delete**.

2. Empty the **Deleted Items** folder.
    a) In the **Folder** pane, right-click the **Deleted Items** folder.
    b) Select **Empty Folder**.
    c) In the Microsoft Outlook dialog box, select **Yes** to permanently delete the items in your **Deleted Items** folder.

Microsoft OneDrive

Microsoft® OneDrive® provides online file storage, management, and sharing services that you can use to store, share, and collaborate on your Office files as well as other types of files. There are two versions of OneDrive: personal and business. Anyone can create a personal OneDrive account, but your organization would provide you with the credentials for a business account. With a OneDrive for Business account, you have up to 1 terabyte (TB) of free OneDrive storage. However, if you have a personal Microsoft account (with an @outlook.com email address), the maximum free storage space is 5 GB. You can certainly purchase additional space if you want to.

Managing your files in OneDrive is very similar to managing files in File Explorer. The major difference is that you must upload the files to OneDrive, which enables you to access and work with your files from nearly any location using different devices. From within the OneDrive browser window, select **Upload** and then navigate to the file you want to upload. You can also upload multiple files at one time by dragging them from **File Explorer** and dropping them in the OneDrive window. While working in a particular Office 2013 application, another way to "upload" a file to OneDrive is to select **File→Save As** and then select **OneDrive** to be the **Save As** location.

Figure 1-18: A sample OneDrive for Business page.

Note: For computers using Windows 8 and older, you will need to download the OneDrive for Business sync client. To do so, follow the **Get the OneDrive apps** link on the OneDrive Home page.

ACTIVITY 1-6
Signing in to Office 365 and OneDrive (Optional Instructor Demo)

Data File

C:\091043Data\Getting Started with Outlook 2013\logo.png

Before You Begin

You have an Office 365 login user name and password.

Scenario

Develetech now uses the Office 2013 applications through their cloud-based Office 365 subscription. While you are becoming comfortable working in the desktop versions of Office, the features of the Office 365 apps are new and unfamiliar. You're especially interested in the collaboration and mobility capabilities of these online apps. After signing in to Office 365, you'll check out the file storage app called OneDrive.

1. From the Windows **Start** screen, open **Internet Explorer** and go to the Office 365 login screen and sign in to Office 365.

   a) Select **Internet Explorer**.

   b) In the **Address** box at the top of the screen, enter *https://login.microsoftonline.com*

2. Enter your credentials to sign in.

   a) In the **User ID** box, enter your user ID, including the @ symbol and the domain name.

   b) In the **Password** box, enter your password.

   c) Select **Sign in**.
      When Office 365 opens, your Outlook mail appears in the Office 365 Outlook app.

   d) Observe the header at the top of the Outlook window.

   When you sign in to your Office 365 account, your Outlook mail is opened first.

3. Open OneDrive.

   a) In the upper-left corner of the window, select the **App Launcher** icon.

   b) From the menu, select the **OneDrive** tile.

4. Install the OneDrive Sync Client on your computer.
   a) In the lower-left corner, select the link **Get the OneDrive apps**.
      When using the Windows 8 operating system, you need to download and install the OneDrive Sync Client that enables you to access and sync your OneDrive files using File Explorer.

    Note: If you are using Windows 10, then the OneDrive Sync Client is included and you won't need to perform this step.

   b) Select **Download** and when prompted, select **Run**.
   c) Follow the prompts to continue the install. You might need to restart the computer.

5. Observe the OneDrive user interface.
   a) In the lower-left corner, select the link **Return to classic OneDrive**.
   b) Observe the OneDrive header.

   The Office 365 header at the top of the screen displays both the App Launcher and OneDrive to indicate that you are working in the online apps. At the right end of the header bar, there are buttons to access **Notifications**, **Settings**, **Help**, and your account settings, from left to right respectively.

   c) Observe the components of the OneDrive window.
      The OneDrive window is divided into two panes. The left side contains a **Search** box and your folder list. The right side contains your **Documents** file list with context-specific commands that are used to create new Office files as well as upload, sync, share, and open files.

    Note: If you have a OneDrive personal account, the text "Office 365" might not appear next to the **App Launcher** icon even though you are accessing it through Office 365.

6. From the student data files, upload the Develetech logo to OneDrive.
   a) From the command bar, select **Upload**.
   b) In the **Choose File to Upload** dialog box, navigate to the **C:\091043Data\Getting Started with Outlook 2013** folder.
   c) Select the **logo.png** image file, and then select **Open**.
   d) Observe the **Documents** list.
      The uploaded Develetech logo image now appears in the **Documents** list.

    Note: You can also use the drag-and-drop method to upload files. To do so, arrange the File Explorer and OneDrive windows so both are visible. In File Explorer, select the desired files and then drag them to the OneDrive window.

   e) Select the check mark column to the left of the file name and observe the available commands.

   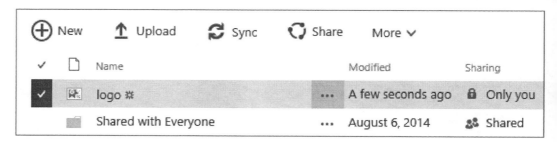

   When a file is selected, file management commands become available. You can use these commands to delete, move, share, or otherwise manage your OneDrive files. You can access additional commands by selecting the **More** button. You can open the selected file in its associated application—either the online or desktop app—from the **More** drop-down menu.

Outlook on the Web

As part of the Office set of apps, Outlook is included in your Office 365 subscription. You can access this scaled-down version of Outlook through your web browser with an Internet connection. You can use Outlook to read and respond to email, organize your messages, and participate in online groups. The type of Office 365 subscription you have—**Business** or **Personal**—will dictate Outlook's appearance and the available features.

- When you sign in to your Office 365 for Business account, you are automatically directed to your Inbox. You will immediately notice that the web-version of Outlook is a simplified version of the Outlook desktop application. However, many of the familiar mail features are available and function the same. You can use the **App Launcher** icon to access tiles for the other Outlook items, such as the **Calendar**, **People**, and **Tasks**.
- You can also access Outlook on the web with a personal Outlook account by signing in with an email address that ends with @outlook.com, @live.com, @hotmail.com, or @msn.com. As expected, your Inbox opens and looks similar to the Outlook for Business interface with a slightly different set of commands. If you are using a free Microsoft account, such as the one shown in the following figure, an advertising pane will appear along the right side of the window.

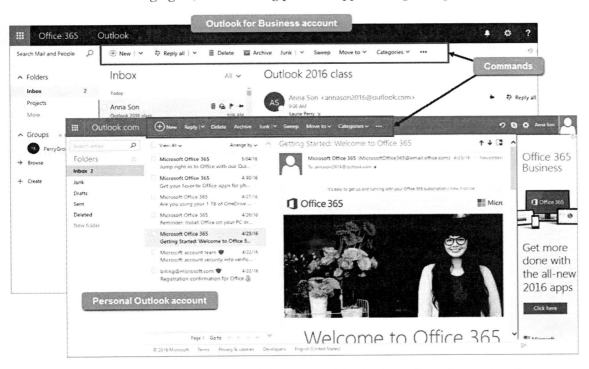

Figure 1–19: The Outlook for Business and the personal Outlook on the web user interfaces.

Some of the major differences between using Outlook 2013 desktop application and Outlook on the web are:

- You must use the **App Launcher** icon ⊞ to navigate to your **Calendar**, **People**, and **Tasks** by selecting the applicable tile.
- Instead of the familiar Office ribbon, commands are located on the task bar as indicated in the previous figure. In online Help, this might also be referred to as the command bar.
- The **Notes** feature is not available from within Outlook; however, you can use the OneNote® Online app that is included in the Office 365 suite of apps.
- The **Clutter** feature is available in both applications, but you must activate it from within Outlook on the web.

ACTIVITY 1-7
Navigating in Outlook on the Web (Optional Instructor Demo)

Before You Begin

You are signed in to Office 365, and Outlook on the web is open.

Scenario

Before you can take full advantage of the collaboration features, you need to familiarize yourself with the Outlook on the web user interface.

1. Open the Outlook web app.

   a) In the upper-left corner of the window, select the **App Launcher** icon.
   b) From the menu, select the **Mail** tile.

   In the web browser, Outlook is quite similar as the desktop application. The window is divided into three panes—**Folder**, **Message List**, and **Reading** pane. At the right end of the Outlook header bar are buttons to access **Notifications**, **Settings**, **Help**, and your account settings, from left to right, respectively. Instead of the familiar Office ribbon, immediately below the Office 365 header are context-specific commands. In Outlook, these commands are used to perform basic mail tasks, such as creating a new message, replying to a message, and archiving a message to name a few.

   c) Observe the **Folders** pane.
   Located along the left side of the window, you can expand and collapse the Inbox folders as you like. You can also access your Outlook groups from this pane as well.

   d) Under **Folders**, select **More** to view additional folders.
   You can now see the complete list of your Outlook folders, including the **Favorites**.

   > **Note:** If you are using a personal Outlook account, the complete list of folders is automatically displayed.

2. Read the messages in the Inbox.

   a) Select any Inbox message.
   b) Observe the command bar.

   When you select a message, the task bar reflects the available actions that you can take.

   c) Read the message text in the **Reading** pane.
   The position of the **Reading** pane can be changed to display across the bottom of the window or hide it completely.

3. Create and send a message to everyone in the class.
    a) In the task bar, select **New**.
        A new message form is displayed in the **Reading** pane. Similar to using the **Pop Out** command, you can select the **Edit in Separate Window** button to open the message form in a new browser window.
    b) In the **To** address field, enter *Class* to send the message to everyone.
    c) In the **Subject** field, enter *Demo Message*
    d) In the message body, type *This message is being composed and sent from Outlook on the web.*
    e) Select the **Send** button.
    f) Ask one of the students to select **Reply all→Reply** to the demo message that they received.

> **Note:** If you select the **Reply all** button, everyone in the address fields will receive your reply. You must intentionally select **Reply** from the drop-down menu to reply to only the sender.

4. Print a selected message.
    a) Select any email message.
    b) In the task bar, select the **More Commands** button. [···]
    c) From the list of commands, select **Print**.
        The selected message is first displayed in a separate browser window and then the **Print** window opens. You can preview the printout and modify the print settings, as desired.
    d) Select **Cancel** to close the Print window.
    e) Close the message window.

5. Use the **App Launcher** to view your calendar, contacts, and tasks.
    a) Select the **App Launcher** icon and then select the **Calendar** tile.

   Rather than selecting an icon from the **Navigation bar**, you access your calendar from the App Launcher. In the Office 365 for Business account, your calendar opens within the same Outlook on the Web window. However, if you are using a personal account, the calendar opens on a new browser tab. The available commands have been reduced to adding new calendar events, sharing, and printing. You can use the commands in the upper-right area of the window to change the calendar view, if desired.

    b) Select the **App Launcher** icon and then select the **People** tile.

   With the exception of the Outlook ribbon, this app containing your personal contacts looks and acts similar to your **Contacts** view in Outlook 2013.

c) Select the **App Launcher** icon and then select the **Tasks** tile.

Again, like the **Tasks** view in the desktop application, your tasks are created and managed in the same way.

 Note: If you are using a personal Office 365 account, you will not have a **Tasks** tile.

d) From the **App Launcher** , select the **Mail** tile.

6. Observe your **Mail** app settings.

a) At the right end of the Office 365 header, select the **Settings** icon. ⚙
Instead of **File** tab and a **Backstage** view, you can use the **Settings** icon to access the Outlook options.

b) Scroll to the bottom of the **Settings** pane and observe the **My app settings** section.

c) Select **Mail**.
Using this link, you can access numerous options to control the automatic processing, account information, and layout settings for your Outlook mail. This is similar to using the **Backstage** view in the desktop application.

7. Access online Help.

a) Select the **Help** icon. **?**
b) In the **Tell Me** box, enter *keyboard shortcuts*
The **Help** pane displays a list of links to suggested help pages.
c) Select one of the suggested links.
The help page opens in a new browser tab.

8. Return to Outlook 2013 to verify that messages exchanged in Outlook on the Web are reflected in the desktop application.

a) Verify that your Outlook on the Web Inbox contains the reply sent from the student.
b) Close the web browser and all open tabs.
c) Switch to Outlook 2013 and point out that the reply sent from the student also appears in the desktop application.

TOPIC C

Use Outlook Help

You know how to navigate the Outlook interface and use the tools available to perform basic email functions, but what if you need assistance with either? In this topic, you will use Outlook **Help**.

Knowing the basics for navigating the Outlook interface and performing some email functions is important to get you started. But what if you forget how to perform an action or want to do something more advanced? Knowing how to access and search Outlook **Help** to find the information you are looking for will help you be more productive when using email to communicate.

Outlook Help

Outlook **Help** is a repository of information regarding the features and functionalities available in Outlook. The Outlook **Help** tool can be accessed whether online or offline. When launched, the Outlook **Help** home window displays links to some commonly accessed help topics about getting started with the Outlook 2013 environment. It also displays common support topics that you can browse through to find information on a specific topic. You can also use the **Instant Search** box to enter a keyword and perform a keyword-specific search.

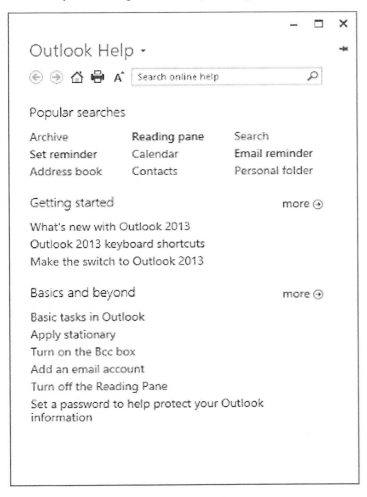

Figure 1–20: The Outlook Help window.

Note: Outlook on the Web

You can access online Help documents by selecting the **Help** icon **?** at the right end of the Office 365 header—immediately to the left of your account profile icon. In the **Help** pane, you can enter a word or phrase in the **Tell Me** box, select one of the suggested help links, or select **Help** at the bottom of the pane to open Outlook on the Web help. Once open, the online app Help window works the same as the desktop application Help window.

Outlook Help Toolbar Buttons

In the Outlook **Help** window, there are a number of toolbar buttons that help you navigate through **Help** or select other options available to you.

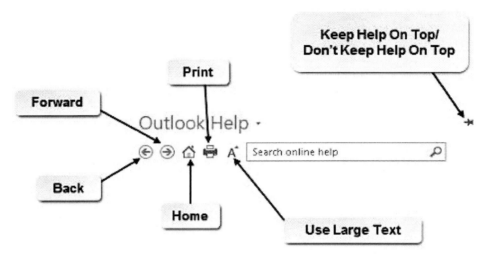

Figure 1–21: The toolbar buttons in the Outlook Help window help you navigate through Help and select the options available.

Toolbar Button	Description
Back	Use the **Back** button to navigate back to the previous page.
Forward	Use the **Forward** button to navigate forward to the next page. This button is only accessible once you have used the **Back** button to visit the previous page; then you can navigate forward to a page you already visited.
Home	Use the **Home** button to return to the home screen of the Outlook **Help** tool.
Print	Use the **Print** button to print the page you are currently viewing.
Use Large Text	Use the **Use Large Text** button to make the text on screen larger than the default size to make it easier to read. Select the button again to return the text to the smaller, default font size.
Keep Help On Top/ Don't Keep Help On Top	Use the **Keep on Top** button to keep the **Help** window on top of other Outlook windows that you have opened. The default setting when you launch **Help** is **Keep on Top**. If you do not want the Outlook **Help** window to display on top of other open Outlook windows, select the button; the button will now be activated and will display as **Not on Top**.

ACTIVITY 1-8
Exploring Outlook Help

Scenario

Since you are new to using Outlook as your email application, there may be some things about it that you aren't comfortable using or need some help with. You want to explore the Outlook **Help** feature to familiarize yourself with it and how it works so you can easily use the **Help** tool when you need it.

1. At the top right of your Outlook window, select the **Microsoft Outlook Help** button to open **Outlook Help**.

2. Search for information using the predefined help topics on the **Help** homepage.
   a) In the **Popular searches** section, select **Email reminder**.
   b) In the list of available help articles, select the article titled **Turn off or postpone a reminder**.
   c) Review the information in the article.
   d) In the toolbar, select the **Home** button ⌂ to return to the homepage.

3. Search for information using the Instant Search box and a keyword.
   a) Place your cursor in the **Instant Search** box, type a keyword or phrase of your choice, and select the **Search** button. 🔍
   b) From the search result list, select an article and review the information.

4. Close the Outlook **Help** window.

Summary

In this lesson, you navigated through the Outlook 2013 interface and used the tools available within it to perform some basic email functions. Knowing your way around the interface and how to complete these basic emailing tasks will allow you to begin working in Outlook immediately.

Which component of the Outlook interface do you think will be most important or useful to you in your everyday life? Why?

What is your own personal experience with using email and a corporate email client like Outlook in a professional setting? Did using email make communicating with your coworkers easier or more difficult?

 Note: Check your CHOICE Course screen for opportunities to interact with your classmates, peers, and the larger CHOICE online community about the topics covered in this course or other topics you are interested in. From the Course screen you can also access available resources for a more continuous learning experience.

2 | Composing Messages

Lesson Time: 1 hour, 15 minutes

Lesson Objectives

In this lesson, you will:

- Create an email message.

- Check spelling and grammar.

- Format message content.

- Attach a file.

- Enhance an email message.

- Manage automatic message content.

Lesson Introduction

Once you are familiar with the Microsoft® Office Outlook® interface and how to use its basic email functions, you are ready to start using Outlook to its fullest capabilities. You are ready to start composing more complex email messages to communicate with others. In this lesson, you will compose messages.

Simply creating a new email and hitting **Send** will get your message to your recipients. But you need to be able to compose an effective email that conveys your message clearly and in a format that doesn't detract from that message. Outlook provides a number of features and functionalities that allow you to compose a sophisticated and meaningful email message.

TOPIC A

Create an Email Message

You don't have to have an address book full of your contacts to create and send an email; you can just type in your recipients' email addresses to send them messages. But what if you do have an easily accessible list of your contacts, where you can select your recipients quickly and conveniently? In this topic, you will select email recipients.

Without having someone to send your messages to, the concept of email is pretty much useless. Determining who you want to send a message to is one of the first steps you will take when composing an email, followed by then selecting those recipients in the message itself. Outlook provides features that can help you quickly and easily select your recipients from a single location, making communicating via email a more streamlined process.

The Address Book

An *address book* in Outlook is a repository for your contacts. Your contacts may include those you have created and saved in Outlook, those you have imported into Outlook from another email client, or those created by your organization. You can use the address book when composing a new message to find and select those contacts to whom you want to send the email message. When you begin typing a recipient's name in the **To** field, Outlook's AutoComplete feature attempts to guess your intended recipient by matching what you're typing with the contacts in your address book. If you have more than one contact in your address book that matches what you're typing, you can use **Ctrl + K** to open the **Check Names** dialog box and manually select the contact from a list.

 Note: You can have more than one address book in Outlook to help you organize your contacts for easy access.

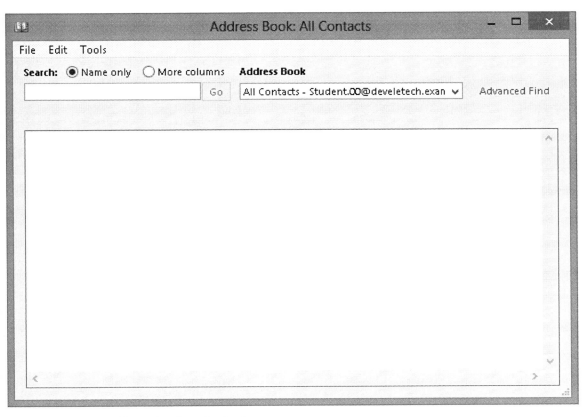

Figure 2-1: The address book in Outlook.

Microsoft Exchange Server

Microsoft Exchange Server is a mail server application that manages the email messages and other types of communications, such as meeting invitations, that are sent through Outlook between users on a network. Microsoft® Exchange Server acts as the communication platform through which all these communications are filtered.

Note: Microsoft Exchange Server is not required for Outlook to manage communications; Outlook can also manage Internet email methods like Post Office Protocol version 3 (POP3) and Internet Message Access Protocol (IMAP). However, if you want users to have access to the same resources such as contacts and meeting information, you will need to use Exchange Server to connect the user accounts in a network. Additionally, some features of Outlook will not be available or function properly without being connected to an Exchange Server.

Global Address List

The *Global Address List* is a list of all users, shared resources, and distribution groups that have been created and networked on the Microsoft Exchange Server for an organization. Global Address Lists are created and maintained by the Exchange administrator. Only users with an email account on the Exchange Server can access a Global Address List.

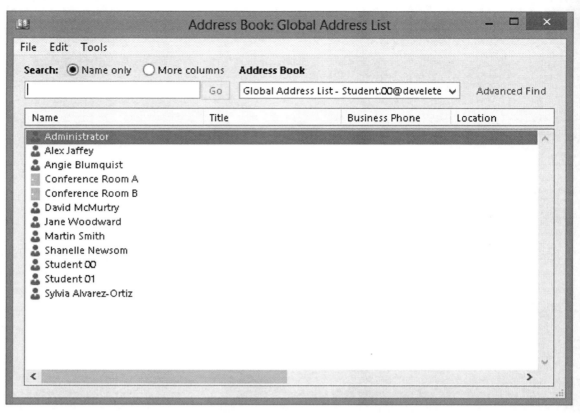

Figure 2-2: A Global Address List in the address book.

Note: If your organization uses a Global Address List, it is likely the default address book that launches when you search for contacts to add to your email messages.

Note: Outlook on the Web

The personal address book and the Global Address List function the same in the online app as they do in the desktop application, including the AutoComplete feature.

MailTips

MailTips is a feature provided when Outlook 2013 is configured with Microsoft Exchange Server 2010 or newer or with Exchange Online. MailTips provide real-time feedback to you concerning the messages you are composing, as they are being composed. As you compose your messages, Outlook and Exchange work together to determine if there are any important notifications you should know about your message, including if you have a large recipient group, if there any issues that may prevent the message from being sent or delivered successfully, or to prevent you from accidentally sending your message to an external recipient. If any issues or important points for notification are detected, the MailTip is displayed between the ribbon and the address fields in your message.

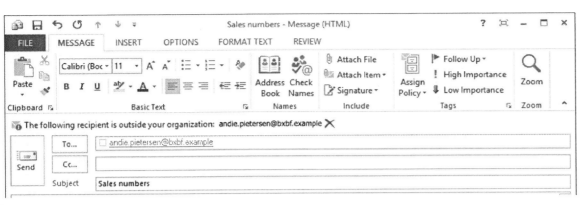

Figure 2-3: MailTips notify you of any issues or important information about your message as you compose it.

MailTips can be turned on or off, and can be configured to only display notifications for certain issues.

 Access the Checklist tile on your CHOICE Course screen for reference information and job aids on How to Create an Email Message.

Beloit College

ACTIVITY 2-1
Creating a New Email Message

Scenario

You have been asked to be one of the lead points of contact for the recruiting efforts at Develetech. Part of your responsibilities will be sending prescreening emails to the recruitment team containing information about each candidate that had applied. You want these emails to be polished and professional, as many people throughout the company will be included on these emails. The first email you will send to the team is about Greg Shannon.

First, you need to select all the appropriate recipients. You want to include the team members as primary recipients, and copy Shanelle Newsom and Angie Blumquist. Then, you will compose an email message that includes the information you want to share about Greg.

---

1. Create a new email message.
   a) In the Outlook window, select **New Email**.

   A new message form window will open.

2. Select the members of the recruitment team, Alex Jaffey, Jane Woodward, and Martin Smith, as your primary recipients using the Global Address List.
   a) Select the **To** button [To...] to open the **Select Names** dialog box.

   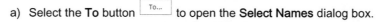
   > **Note:** The dialog box automatically defaults to a name only search within the Global Address List as the address book. Verify that these options are chosen.

   b) In the list of names, find and select **Alex Jaffey** and select the **To** button. [To ->]
   c) In the list of names, find and select **Jane Woodward** and select the **To** button.
   d) In the list of names, find and select **Martin Smith** and select the **To** button.

3. Copy Shanelle Newsom and Angie Blumquist on the message using the Global Address List.
   a) In the **Select Names** dialog box, find and select **Shanelle Newsom** and select the **CC** button.

   b) In the list of names, find and select **Angie Blumquist** and select the **CC** button.
   c) Select **OK**.

4. Enter the subject line for the email message.
   a) Place your cursor in the **Subject** field in the message form and type *Greg Shannon prescreen information*
   b) Place your cursor in the message body and notice that the title bar of the message changes to "Greg Shannon: prescreen information - Message (HTML)."

5. Enter your message content in the message body.

a) In the message body, type *Here is some information about Greg Shannon. Greg has a lot of experience in mnay related fields.*

 Caution: Type the text in the message body as indicated, even with the typographical errors. These errors will be fixed when you check for spelling and grammar.

b) Press **Enter** twice to place two hard returns in the email message.

c) Type *Gregs resune is attached. Please look it over and let me know by tomorrow if you think it is worth having Greg come in for an interview.*

 Caution: Type the text in the message body as indicated, even with the typographical errors. These errors will be fixed when you check for spelling and grammar.

TOPIC B

Check Spelling and Grammar

You have added text into your message and have formatted the message content to your liking. Before sending any message, it is a good idea to make sure that your message is free of any egregious errors. In this topic, you will check spelling and grammar in your message.

You're only human, and humans make mistakes. Whether entering a quick message to a friend or composing a complex email to a coworker or boss, it is highly likely that you will make some mistakes in your spelling or grammar usage within your message content. Sending a message with errors can detract from the message you are trying to convey and, worse, make you look unprofessional. Using the spelling and grammar tools provided in Outlook 2013 prevents any unwanted and potentially embarrassing errors in your email messages.

The AutoCorrect Feature

The *AutoCorrect* feature is a tool in Outlook that checks for common typing errors, including spelling and grammar errors, capitalization mistakes, and other typographical mistakes. By default, spelling and grammar are automatically checked as you type your message. If you make a mistake while typing and AutoCorrect can determine what was intended, it will automatically correct the error. For more complicated mistakes that AutoCorrect cannot fix automatically, it will notify you visually in the message that there is an error using wavy underlines of various colors; wavy red underlines indicate a possible spelling error, wavy blue underlines indicate a possible word choice error, and wavy green underlines indicate a possible grammatical error.

When AutoCorrect notifies you that there is a possible error, you can right-click on the word or words with the error, and AutoCorrect will provide you with a list of possible corrections. Within this list, you can also choose to ignore the correction, add the word to your AutoCorrect dictionary, or configure AutoCorrect options.

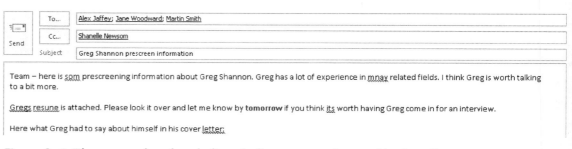

Figure 2-4: The wavy colored underlines indicate errors detected by AutoCorrect.

> **Note: Outlook on the Web**
>
> In the online app, there is no **Spelling and Grammar** dialog box or a command to access it; however, the **AutoCorrect** feature will indicate incorrect words with red, wavy underlines.

The Spelling and Grammar Checker

Outlook comes with a Spelling and Grammar checker that you can use to detect spelling and grammatical errors in your email message before you send it. When you have completed composing your message, you can run the Spelling and Grammar checker, which is located on the **REVIEW** tab of the ribbon. If there are any spelling or grammar errors in your email message detected during the Spelling and Grammar check, the **Spelling and Grammar** dialog box will display. For each of the errors detected, the **Spelling and Grammar** dialog box provides a suggestion for how to correct the error.

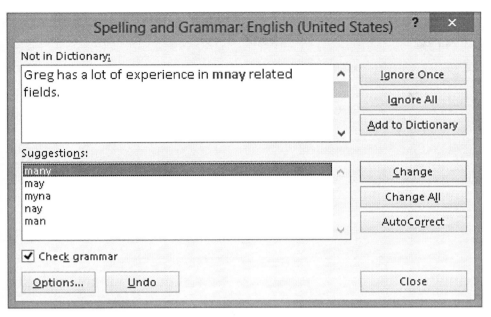

Figure 2-5: The Spelling and Grammar dialog box appears if there are any spelling or grammar errors detected.

If there are no errors or once you have addressed all the detected errors in the email, Outlook will notify you that the spelling and grammar check is complete.

Components of the Spelling and Grammar Dialog Box

The Spelling and Grammar dialog box has a number of components and accompanying actions to use to correct mistakes in your email messages.

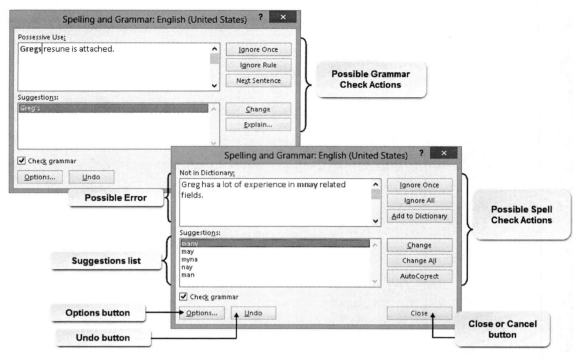

Figure 2-6: The components and options in the Spelling and Grammar dialog box.

Dialog Box Component	Description
Possible error	The top section of the dialog box displays the possible error that the Spelling and Grammar check has identified, which may include any words that you have misspelled, possible word choice errors, or grammatical errors.
Suggestions	The **Suggestions** section lists possible words that you intended to type, the correct spelling of a misspelled word, or the correct grammar usage for a grammatical error.
Possible spell check actions	For the word that has been detected as misspelled and is displayed in the **Not in Dictionary** section, there are a number of actions you can choose to take based on the error and suggestion: • **Ignore Once:** Ignores the spelling error. It will advance you to the next error, if there are any further errors. • **Ignore All:** Ignores all instances of spelling errors that were detected, and ends the spelling and grammar check. • **Add to Dictionary:** If the word that has been detected as an error is actually correct (such a term commonly used in your specific business), you can add the word to your dictionary. It will not change the word in your current message, and will not detect it as an error in future spelling and grammar checks. • **Change:** Changes the spelling of the word to the option from the Suggestions list that you have chosen. • **Change All:** Changes all instances of spelling errors that were detected to an option from the Suggestions list. • **AutoCorrect:** Will apply the AutoCorrect option. If there is a word that you know you often misspell, you can use AutoCorrect to correct the word in this instance to the suggested change, and Outlook will save the suggested option and automatically change it to that option every time you misspell the word.

Dialog Box Component	Description
Possible grammar check actions	For the phrase that has been detected as grammatically incorrect and is displayed in the Not in Dictionary section, there are a number of actions you can choose to take based on the error and suggestion: • **Ignore Once:** Ignores the grammar error and the suggested change. It will advance you to the next error, if there are any further errors. If you run the Spelling and Grammar check again, this error will be detected again. • **Ignore Rule:** Ignores the error and the suggested change, and ignores the rule for that error. It will advance you to the next error, if there are any further errors. If you run the Spelling and Grammar check again, this error will not be detected again. • **Next Sentence:** Advances to the next sentence without applying any changes to the message. It will advance you to the next error, if there are any further errors. If you run the Spelling and Grammar check again, this error will be detected again. • **Change:** Changes the grammatically incorrect phrase to the correct option from the **Suggestions** list that you have chosen. • **Explain:** If you are not sure why the phrase is grammatically incorrect, Explain will tell you which grammar or usage rule has been violated.
Options	The **Options** button open the **Editor Options** dialog box, where you can specify settings and options for how spelling and grammatical errors are handled.
Undo	The **Undo** button undoes the last action that you performed in the spelling and grammar check.
Close or Cancel	The **Close** or **Cancel** button cancels the spelling and grammar check, and closes the dialog box. Depending on the actions you have previously taken within the dialog box, this button will change to reflect an appropriate action that can be taken, **Close** or **Cancel**.

Note: When you use **Change** or **Change All,** unless you select an option in the **Suggestions** list directly, it will replace the error with the first suggestion in the list. Be mindful that this suggested change is really what you want to change your word or phrase to.

Access the Checklist tile on your CHOICE Course screen for reference information and job aids on How to Check Spelling and Grammar.

ACTIVITY 2-2
Checking Spelling and Grammar in a Message

Scenario

Now that you have composed the text in your email about Greg Shannon to share with the other members of the recruitment team, you want to check the content for any spelling or grammar errors. You don't want to send the email to your teammates with any mistakes, which would make you look unprofessional. You will use the Spelling and Grammar check in Outlook to double-check your email message.

1. Run the Spelling and Grammar check on your message content.
   a) In the message form, place your cursor at the beginning of the message content.
   b) On the ribbon, select the **REVIEW** tab.
   c) Select the **Spelling & Grammar** command.

   Spelling &
   Grammar

2. Correct the errors detected in the Spelling and Grammar check.
   a) In the **Spelling and Grammar: English (U.S)** dialog box, in the **Not in Dictionary** section, verify that the word "mnay" is highlighted in red, indicating a misspelling.
   b) In the **Suggestions** section, verify that the word **many** is selected, and select **Change**.
   c) In the **Not in Dictionary** section, verify that the word "Gregs" is highlighted in red, indicating a misspelling.
   d) In the **Suggestions** section, verify that the word **Greg's** is selected, and select **Change**.
   e) In the **Not in Dictionary** section, verify that the word "resune" is highlighted in red, indicating a misspelling.
   f) In the **Suggestions** section, select **résumé,** and select **Change**.
   g) In the **Microsoft Outlook** dialog box telling you that the spelling and grammar check is complete, select **OK**.

TOPIC C

Format Message Content

When you create and send a basic email, you might just find yourself typing your message content into the message body. But, what if you have text you want to paste into your message from another document, that perhaps has different formatting? In this topic, you will format message content.

When you send a basic email message, you might not be too concerned about how your message content is formatted. But as you begin to work with more complex message content, especially in a business setting, you may find you need to format your message content for consistency or professional appearance. Outlook provides a number of tools to help you format your message content to help you create polished, professional-looking emails.

Message Formats

Email messages can be sent in different formats: Hyper Text Markup Language (HTML), the primary language used to write web content; Rich Text Format (RTF), a Microsoft-specific format; and plain text. HTML and RTF messages can be formatted with traditional document options, such as fonts, colors, bulleted lists, and images. Plain text messages cannot be formatted with any of these text formatting options.

Not all email clients support all of these formats; while most email applications support HTML, plain text is the only format that is supported by all applications. RTF is only supported by Microsoft email clients.

> **Note: Outlook on the Web**
> When composing a new message, you can select the **More commands** button to switch between HTML and plain text formats.

> **Access the Checklist tile on your CHOICE Course screen for reference information and job aids on How to Change Message Format.**

Paste Options

Outlook 2013, like many other Microsoft Office applications, provides a number of paste options that you can use when copying and pasting text or objects from another location into your message content. There are three paste options that might be used to paste content into your message body.

Paste Option	Description
	Keep Source Formatting: the content, when pasted into the message body, retains the formatting from the original source content.
	Merge Formatting: the content, when pasted into the message body, adapts the formatting of the location or document where it has been pasted.
	Keep Text Only: the content, when pasted into the message body, is pasted without any formatting or graphics at all, and is simply pasted as plain text.

The paste options can be accessed either by right-clicking in the message body to open the contextual menu or by clicking the **Paste** command in the **Clipboard** command group in either the **MESSAGE** or **FORMAT TEXT** tabs on the ribbon.

Note: You must copy the content you want to paste into your message before selecting your paste options. Depending on the content you have copied, different paste options will be available to use.

Use Destination Theme Paste Option

If content has been copied from a source that has been formatted with styles or themes, the **Use Destination Theme** paste option will also be available. The content, when pasted into the message body, retains the style name that was applied to the text in the original source, but uses the style definition of the message where the text was pasted.

Paste Special Option

The **Paste Special** option lets you select a more specific format for content that you are pasting into your message body. **Paste Special** can only be accessed by clicking the **Paste** command in the **Clipboard** command group in either the **MESSAGE** or **FORMAT TEXT** tabs on the ribbon. When you select this paste option, the **Paste Special** dialog box appears, where you can select the desired format for your text. The formats available depend on the content that has been copied and what formats the application supports where it is being pasted.

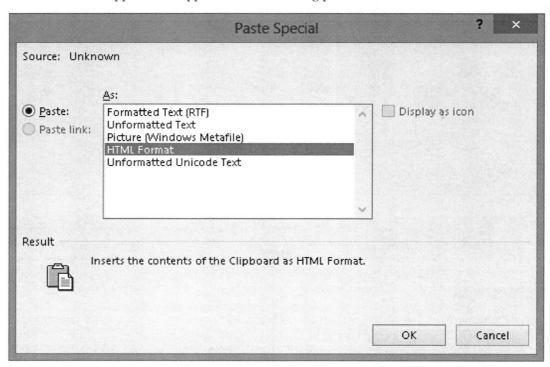

Figure 2-7: The Paste Special option lets you select from a variety of supported formats.

 Note: Outlook on the Web

In the online app, the available paste options are **Paste as is**, **Paste simple HTML**, and **Paste text**.

Live Preview

Live Preview is a feature in Outlook 2013 and other Office 2013 products that provides you with a sneak peek of what your formatting changes will look like if they were applied before actually applying those changes. When you are making formatting changes to your message content, you can hover over a formatting command either on the ribbon or the contextual menu. If Live Preview is available for that option, a preview of your text with that formatting option applied will appear in your message body. You can then select the formatting option that best suits your needs or preferences.

 Note: Live Preview applies to a number of formatting and enhancement options in Outlook, mostly related to Styles and Themes. More information about Styles can be found later on in this lesson.

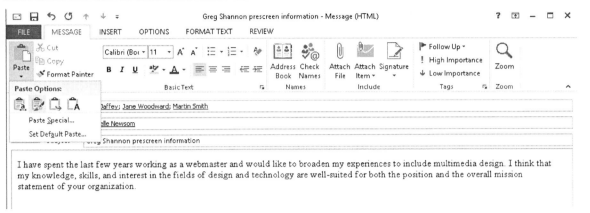

Figure 2-8: Live Preview displays the results of applying the Keep Source Formatting paste option to message content.

 Note: Outlook on the Web

This feature is not available in the online app; however, you can open the message in Outlook 2013 to use the Live Preview feature.

The Mini Toolbar

The *Mini toolbar* is a floating toolbar that appears when text has been selected in the body of your Outlook message. When you hover your pointer over the selected text, the Mini toolbar appears; when you move off of the selected text, the Mini toolbar disappears.

The Mini toolbar features tools that are commonly used for text formatting, without having to access these tools from the ribbon. The tools in the Mini toolbar include:

- Basic font options such as font type, font size, grow font/shrink font, and font color.
- Text formatting options such as bold, italics, or underline.
- Paragraph formatting options such as bullet or numbered lists.
- Text highlighting colors options.
- Format painter, which can be used to copy formatting from one place and apply it to text selected elsewhere.
- Styles that can be applied to the selected text.

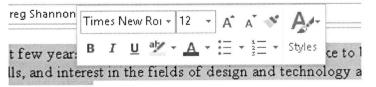

Figure 2-9: The Mini toolbar displays text formatting options for selected text.

Note: Outlook on the Web

This formatting toolbar is also available in the online app; however, there are fewer buttons and they are slightly different in appearance. In addition to the toolbar that appears when text is selected, you can also use the formatting tools located at the bottom of the message area.

Access the Checklist tile on your CHOICE Course screen for reference information and job aids on How to Format Message Content.

ACTIVITY 2-3
Formatting Message Content

Data File

C:\091043Data\Composing Messages\Greg Shannon Cover Letter.docx

Before You Begin

Microsoft Word 2013 has been installed on your machine.

Scenario

You have selected the appropriate recipients, composed the message body, and checked the spelling and grammar for your prescreening email about Greg Shannon to send to the recruitment team. Because this email requires their attention and a response, you also want to make sure that the email is formatted well so that the members of the team can read and respond to it quickly and easily. You especially want to emphasize that you need the team members to respond by tomorrow at the latest.

Part of your message will include a portion of Greg's cover letter to share with the rest of the team, rather than including the whole document for them to read on their own. You will paste this into the email message and make sure it is formatted in the way you want it to be.

---

1. Enter some introductory text before where you paste the portion of Greg's cover letter.
   a) Select at the end of the second paragraph of text.
   b) Press **Enter** twice to place two hard returns in the email message.
   c) Type *Here is what Greg had to say about himself in his cover letter:*

2. Format the message content you composed using the Mini toolbar.
   a) Select and highlight all of the text in the message body. The Mini toolbar will appear above the highlighted text.

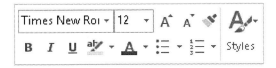

 Note: If you move your cursor away from the highlighted text, the Mini toolbar will turn translucent and then disappear. If the Mini toolbar is translucent, you can hover your cursor over it to make it appear fully and use the toolbar. If it disappears, you will need to select the text again to make it reappear.

   b) In the Mini toolbar, from the **Font** drop-down, find and select **Lucida Sans Unicode**.
   c) Select the **Decrease Font Size** button A once to shrink the font to 10 point size.
   d) In the message body, select only the word "tomorrow" in the second paragraph. The Mini toolbar will appear above the text.
   e) Move the cursor over the Mini toolbar until it appears fully.
   f) Select the **Bold** button B to bold the word.

g) Select the **Font Color** down-arrow and in the **Standard Colors** section, select **Dark Red,** the first color from the left in the bottom row.

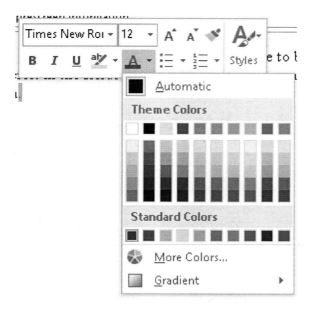

3. Copy and paste a portion of Greg's cover letter into the message body.

a) Minimize the Greg Shannon: prescreen information - Message (HTML) window and the Microsoft Outlook window.

b) Navigate to the **C:\091043Data\Composing Messages** folder.

c) Open **Greg Shannon Cover Letter.docx**.

d) Select and copy the third full paragraph in the document, starting with "I have spent..."

e) Maximize the Microsoft Outlook window and then the Greg Shannon: prescreen information - Message (HTML) window.

f) Place your cursor in the message body after the "Here is what Greg had to say about himself in his cover letter:" and press **Enter** twice to insert two hard returns.

g) On the ribbon, from either the **MESSAGE** or the **FORMAT TEXT** tab, select the **Paste** option down-arrow.

h) Hover over the paste options buttons and view the paste text as it would appear in the message using Live Preview.

i) Select the second button from the left, **Keep Source Formatting** to paste the content with the formatting from the original document.

4. Close the **Greg Shannon Cover Letter** Word document.

TOPIC D

Attach Files and Items

Now that you have selected your recipients, composed and formatted your message, and possibly checked for spelling and grammar, you are ready to send your message. But what if there is other information you want to include with your message, such as a document or file? In this topic, you will attach a file to an email message.

Sometimes, you may have information that you want to include in your message that cannot be included in the message body. Perhaps you have been working on a document and want to share that document with others for their input or feedback. Rather than pasting the text from that document into your email, you can attach that document to the email for all your recipients to read and review at their convenience.

Attachments

An *attachment* is a document or file that is included and sent along with your email message. A message in the Inbox with the **Paperclip** icon next to it indicates that the message contains an attachment.

Figure 2-10: The Paperclip icon indicates there is an attachment.

Depending on the message format, the actual attached document will appear in a different location. For HTML or plain text messages, the attachment will appear in a separate **Attached** field beneath the **Subject** field of the email. It will include the file name and type and the file size. For RTF messages, the attachment will appear in the body of the message content. It will display as the **File Type** icon and will include the file name.

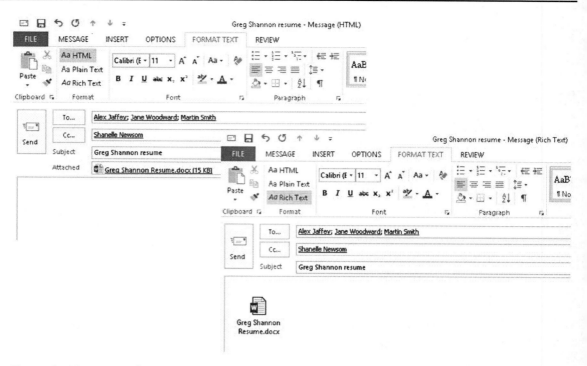

Figure 2-11: An attachment appears in a separate attachment line in an HTML or plain text message, while it appears in the body of the message in an RTF message.

Note: Outlook on the Web

In the online app, you can attach files in the traditional way as a copy or as a linked file that is shared via OneDrive®. The recipient will need to sign in to their Microsoft account (or create an account) before they can view the linked attachment.

File Type and Size for Attachments

When sending a file as an attachment, the file type and file size are important factors. Some guidelines you should follow for including attachments in your mail messages include:

- Be conscious of the type of file that you are sending. Not all recipients may have the application needed to open and read an attached file. For instance, most recipients will be able to open and read a .pdf file that has been attached, as PDF readers are easily accessible. However, most recipients would not be able to open and read an .ind file, as most will not have the Adobe® InDesign® application that would be needed to handle a native file type. Make sure to attach a file type that your recipients will be able to manage.

- Be conscious of the size of the file that you are sending. Large attachments require a lot of space and can clog a recipient's Inbox; in some cases, when an Inbox has reached or exceeded a maximum amount of file space being used, it will stop receiving messages. Some organizations limit the file size for attachments that can be sent or received to prevent this from happening. Make sure to attach files that are small enough for your recipients to be able to manage.

Note: If you do need to send large files, you may have to send them in multiple messages or look into an alternative way of sharing files, such as an online drop box or File Transfer Protocol (FTP) site.

Outlook Items as Attachments

Outlook items can be attached to your email messages and sent to other recipients. Attaching Outlook items can make it easier to share multiple messages, contacts, tasks, a view of your calendar, and even specific calendar events with others.

Note: While you can send Outlook items to recipients outside your organization who are not using Outlook themselves, not all files will necessarily be compatible with other email clients. Attaching Outlook items works best between users on the same domain, and with recipients using Exchange Server and Outlook.

You can use the commands in the **Include** command group on the **INSERT** tab to attach different Outlook items.

Figure 2-12: The commands to attach Outlook Items to an email message on the INSERT tab.

Attached Item	Description
Outlook Item	You can attach an Outlook item such as an email message, meeting invite, or task. When attaching one of these items, you can choose to insert the item as an attachment or as text only, which will appear in the message body. Those who use Outlook should be able to open, save, and interact with these attachments; those using another email client should be able to view the text in the message body, but may not be able to interact directly with the attached file.
Business Card	You can attach a business card with contact information for one or more of your contacts. Along with the file being attached, a view of the business card will display in the message body. Those who use Outlook can view the file and even save it to their own contacts. Those not using Outlook may not be able to interact with the item directly, such as opening or saving the file.
Calendar	You can attach a link to your calendar with information about your meeting events. Along with the link to your calendar, a view of your calendar for a specific date range and with the level of detail of your choice will display in the message body. Those who use Outlook can use the link to open and view your calendar. Those not using Outlook may not be able to interact with the item directly, such as opening and viewing the calendar.

 Note: Outlook on the Web

Attaching Outlook items is not available in the online app. To use these options, you must use the desktop application.

Attachment Reminder

Outlook 2013 can detect if an attachment was omitted from a message and notify you that the attachment is missing. Outlook will scan messages before they are sent and look for any indications that you intended to attach a document, such as the word "attachment" in the subject or message text. When Outlook detects that you may have forgotten an attachment, it will display the **Attachment Reminder** dialog box before sending the message.

By default, the Attachment Reminder is enabled in Outlook 2013.

Attachment Reminder

You may have forgotten to attach a file.

☐ Don't show this message again

| Don't Send | Send Anyway |

Figure 2-13: The Attachment Reminder dialog box.

 Access the Checklist tile on your CHOICE Course screen for reference information and job aids on How to Attach Files and Items.

ACTIVITY 2-4
Attaching a File to a Message

Data File

C:\091043Data\Composing Messages\Greg Shannon Resume.docx

Scenario

In your email message to the recruitment team working on screening potential candidates, you provided a little bit of information about Greg Shannon from his cover letter. You decided to attach Greg's résumé to send to the team so that they could all review it on their own time. You need to attach the file to the email message to the recruitment team.

Attach Greg Shannon's résumé to your email message.

a) Select the **MESSAGE** tab, and in the **Include** command group, select **Attach File**.

Attach
File

b) In the **Insert File** dialog box, navigate to the **C:\091043Data\Composing Messages** folder.
c) Select **Greg Shannon Resume.docx**.
d) Select **Insert**.
e) Verify that in the **Message** form, below the **Subject** line, the **Attached** field is now displayed, where the file icon, name, and size of the attached file are displayed.

TOPIC E

Enhance an Email Message

Once you have added the necessary pieces into your email—your recipients, your message content, any attachments—now you can have some fun making your emails look unique. Outlook provides a number of features and tools to add images, themes, styles, and more to modify the appearance of your emails. In this topic, you will enhance an email message.

Outlook provides features like themes, styles, and SmartArt that can be added to your emails to make them more visually pleasing, polished, or professional-looking. You can use the features and tools provided in Outlook to enhance your email messages and convey your messages more effectively, while being more aesthetically pleasing.

Note: Outlook on the Web

In the online app, you can insert pictures and Emojis (small icons used to convey emotion) into your messages. To insert any of the other illustrations covered in this topic, you must use the desktop application. However, when you receive messages that contain illustrations, you will be able to see any shapes, SmartArt, charts, and screenshots that have been inserted.

The Illustrations Command Group

The **Illustrations** command group, found on the **INSERT** tab of the ribbon in a message form, includes the commands you can use for inserting various graphical elements into your email messages.

Figure 2-14: The Illustrations command group includes commands for inserting various graphical elements into your message.

The graphical elements that can be inserted into a message include:

- **Pictures**
- **Online Pictures**
- **Shapes**
- **SmartArt**
- **Chart**
- **Screenshot**

Note: Pictures are inserted from an external source, such as images that have been saved to your local computer. The Online Pictures option allows you to search a variety of online sources provided by Outlook to find and insert an image that suits your needs.

SmartArt

SmartArt is a tool provided in Outlook and many other Office 2013 applications that lets you format your information into a graphical representation to help convey your message and hopefully help those receiving the message to remember and recall that information. SmartArt graphics organize your information into a graphical layout that effectively communicates your idea and can be easily understood.

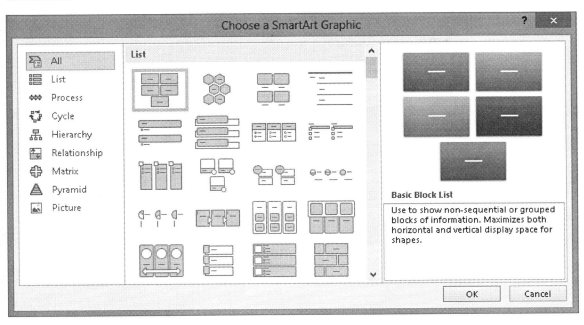

Figure 2-15: SmartArt graphics can organize your information into a number of visual style options that help people understand your message.

There are a number of SmartArt types that can be applied to your information:

- **List** displays your information as items in a list using graphics.
- **Process** displays your information as a series of steps in a process, such as a flowchart.
- **Cycle** displays your information as a sequence of stages in a cycle, such as a lifecycle.
- **Hierarchy** displays your information as a series of hierarchical relationships, such as an organizational chart.
- **Relationship** displays your information as a series of related pieces, such as a Venn diagram.
- **Matrix** displays your information as parts that make up a whole, such as quadrants of a whole.
- **Pyramid** displays your information relationally or hierarchically where components are building in size, such as an inverted pyramid.
- **Picture** displays your information using a graphical representation, such as an image with callouts.

 Note: For a complete description and an example of all the SmartArt types and graphics available, visit Outlook Help and search for descriptions of SmartArt graphics.

Each SmartArt graphic is editable and customizable, so you can add your own text, colors, and add, remove, move, or resize shapes as needed.

The Screenshot Tool

The **Screenshot** tool in Outlook is used to capture an image of the screen for any open and available window on your desktop. When you open the **Screenshot** tool, you can choose to capture the entire image of one of your open windows, or you can use the **Screen Clipping** tool to select just part of a screen to capture.

When a screenshot is captured, it is automatically inserted into the message body of your email message.

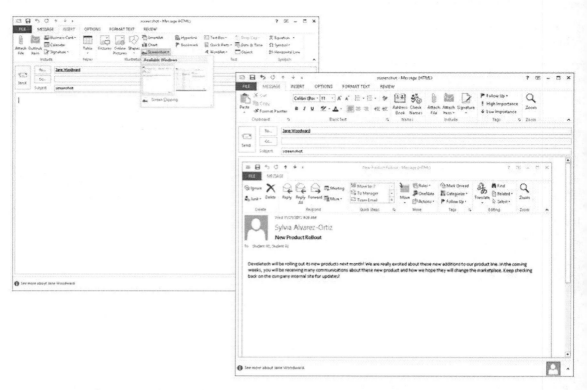

Figure 2-16: The Screenshot Tool captures an image of an available screen on your desktop and inserts it in your email message.

The Text Command Group

The **Text** command group, found on the **INSERT** tab of the ribbon in a message form, includes the commands you can use for inserting various graphical text elements into your email messages.

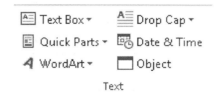

Figure 2-17: Text commands are available for inserting various graphical text elements into your email messages.

The graphical text elements that can be inserted into a message include:

* **Text Box**
* **Quick Parts**
* **WordArt**
* **Drop Cap**
* **Date & Time**
* **Object**

 Note: Object allows you to insert any number of other types of files or objects, including video clips, audio clips, and documents from other Microsoft applications.

Quick Parts

Quick Parts is a feature in Outlook that lets you create, save, and reuse pieces of content that you use often, including document titles, author names, and AutoText. AutoText is another feature of Outlook that lets you save and reuse words or phrases that you use often; they are added to the AutoText gallery for you to access and insert into an email quickly and easily.

WordArt

WordArt is a text-styling feature that allows you to insert and modify text in your email using special effects. WordArt effects include colored outlines, colored fill, and text effects like shadowing, 3-D rotation, and other transform effects.

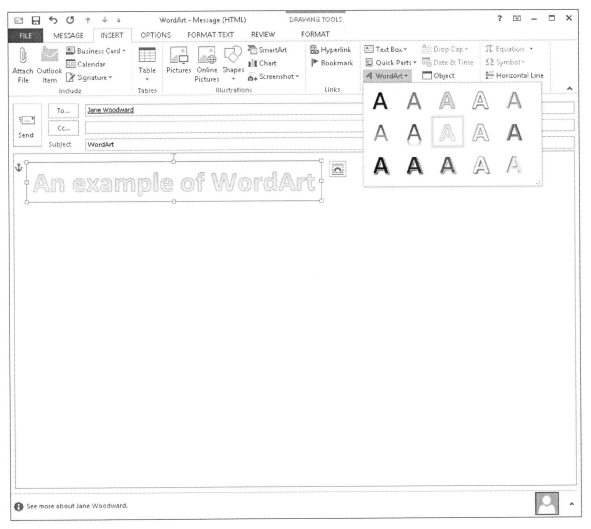

Figure 2-18: WordArt that has been inserted in an email can be modified using the various text effects available.

Contextual Tabs

Contextual tabs are additional tabs that become available on the ribbon when you insert a graphical object or select a graphical object you have inserted into an email message. They are displayed to the right of the typical tabs on the ribbon. The contextual tabs provide commands and options specific to the type of object you have inserted, and are used to edit, manipulate, or customize the graphic element.

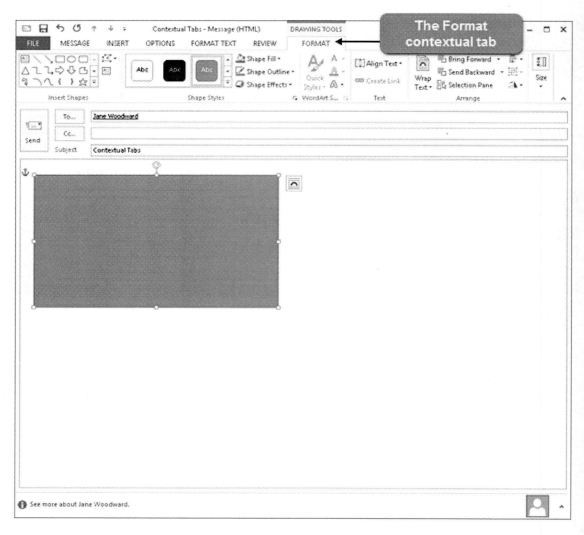

Figure 2-19: The contextual tabs appear on the ribbon when a graphical object is inserted or selected.

Depending on the type of illustration selected, the contextual tab that appears may differ.

- The **FORMAT** contextual tab appears when you have inserted or selected a picture, clip art, shape, SmartArt, or screenshot into your email message. The **FORMAT** tab provides commands for formatting these objects, such as modifying the appearance of the object, applying effects to the object, cropping the size of the object, adjusting the position of the object in the message, and so on.
- The **DESIGN** contextual tab appears when you have inserted or selected SmartArt into your email message. The **DESIGN** tab provides commands for applying changes to the design and layout of the SmartArt object, such as creating and modifying the graphics in the object, applying specific SmartArt Layouts, changing the color of the SmartArt object, and so on.

The Layout Contextual Tab

There is a third contextual tab, the **LAYOUT** tab, that appears when you insert or select tables and charts in your email message.

Contextual Tool Tabs

The contextual tabs that are available for a specific object type will be grouped together in a contextual tool tab. They are called out in the title bar above the ribbon with the appropriate title. The title bar also changes color in the are surrounding the contextual tabs that it contains. The contextual tool tabs that will appear when working with illustrations or text include:

- **PICTURE TOOLS**
- **DRAWING TOOLS**
- **SMARTART TOOLS**

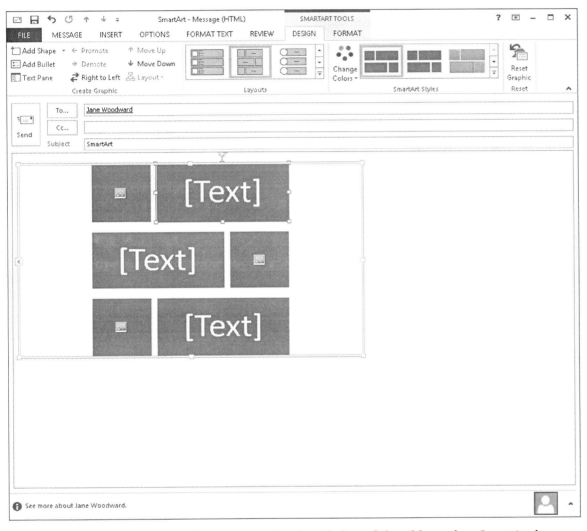

Figure 2-20: The SmartArt Tools tab appears in the title bar of the ribbon when SmartArt has been inserted or selected.

The Background Removal Tool

The **Background Removal** tool, launched by selecting the **Remove Background** command on the **FORMAT** contextual tab of the **PICTURE TOOLS** tab, allows you to remove the background from an image you have inserted, leaving just the part of the picture containing an image object.

You can use the tools in **Background Removal** to select the areas to keep and the areas to remove.

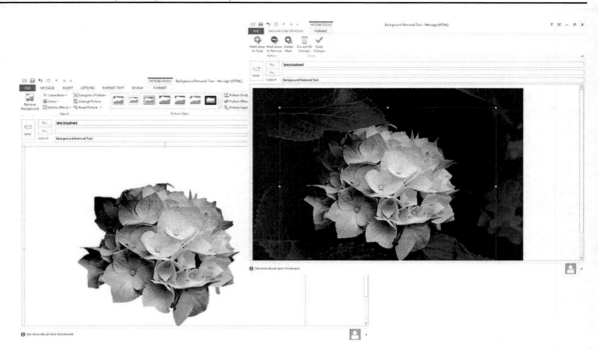

Figure 2-21: The Background Removal tool lets you select areas of the background to keep or remove from your image.

Galleries

A *gallery* is a library of all the options that are available for a specific command. If there are many items that can be inserted or formatting options that can be applied, those options are listed in the gallery for that command.

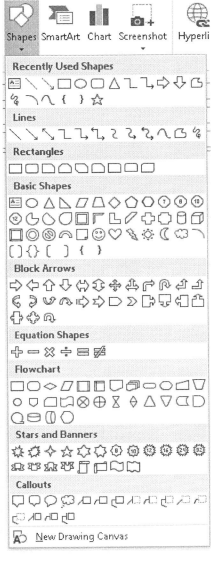

Figure 2-22: The gallery of shapes that can be inserted appears when the Shapes command is selected.

 Access the Checklist tile on your CHOICE Course screen for reference information and job aids on How to Use Graphical Elements To Enhance a Message.

ACTIVITY 2-5
Enhancing an Email Message with an Image

Data File

C:\091043Data\Composing Messages\Greg Shannon Icon Samples.png

Scenario

You have decided that you want to include a sample of a Greg Shannon's graphic design work in the prescreening email to the recruitment team. You have chosen an icon that Greg has created and included in his portfolio of work to use as a sample. You want to insert it into the email as an image so the team can see the sample, without having to open an attachment.

---

1. Insert Greg's sample icon as a picture file in the email message.
   a) In the message body, place your cursor at the end of the last sentence of text.
   b) Press **Enter** twice to place two hard returns in the email message.
   c) Type *Here is a small sample of some of Greg's work:*

    Note: If you see that the new sentence inherited the formatting of the paragraph you copied and pasted from Greg's resume earlier, select the new sentence, select the **FORMAT TEXT** tab, locate the **Styles** command group, and select the **Normal** style.

   d) Press **Enter** twice to place two hard returns in the email message.
   e) Select the **INSERT** tab, and in the **Illustrations** command group, select **Pictures**.
   f) In the **Insert Picture** dialog box, navigate to the **C:\091043Data\Composing Messages** folder.
   g) Select **Greg Shannon Icon Samples.png**.
   h) Select **Insert**.
   i) Verify that the sample icon was placed in the message body.

2. Compress the picture file.
   a) If necessary, in the message body, select the picture. The **PICTURE TOOLS** contextual tab appears.
   b) On the **FORMAT** tab, in the **Adjust** command group, select the **Compress Pictures** button.
   c) In the **Compress Pictures** dialog box, verify that the **Apply only to this picture check box** is checked.
   d) In the **Target output** section, select the **E-mail (96ppi)** radio button and select **OK**.

Styles

Styles are a set of preconfigured formatting options that are included in Outlook 2013. A style may be comprised of formatting options such as font type, font color, paragraph spacing, and more. There are a number of preconfigured styles available to apply to your text, and you can edit these styles or create new ones to suit your needs.

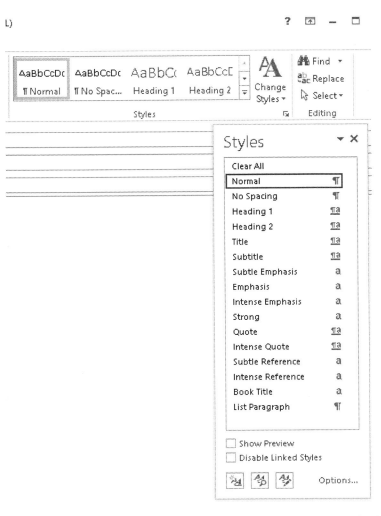

Figure 2-23: Styles that are available in Outlook can be applied to your message content to quickly make formatting changes.

 Access the Checklist tile on your **CHOICE** Course screen for reference information and job aids on **How to Use Styles To Enhance a Message.**

Themes

Themes are preconfigured design and formatting options that can be applied to your message to ensure consistency in all content that you create or place in the message body. The theme that is selected specifies the font types that will be used for text in the message, the colors that can be used in the message, and the effects that can be applied to any graphical elements like shapes that are inserted into the message.

There are several themes that are included with the Outlook application. Themes are found on the **OPTIONS** tab of the ribbon. You can also customize the existing themes to suit your own personal needs.

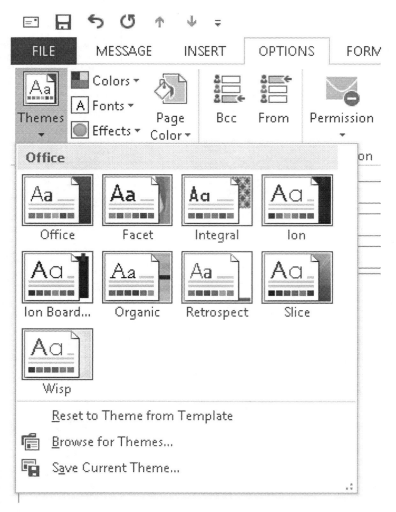

Figure 2-24: The Themes gallery displays the preconfigured design and formatting options that can be applied to your email message.

 Access the Checklist tile on your CHOICE Course screen for reference information and job aids on How to Use Themes to Enhance a Message.

ACTIVITY 2-6
Enhancing an Email Message with SmartArt and Themes

Scenario

You want to include a brief description of the hiring process to the team in your email. Using a SmartArt graphic will be a simple way to show the team what will be happening in the process over the next few weeks. Then you will apply a theme to your SmartArt to make it look more professional. With all your enhancements included, you can finally send your message to the recruitment team.

1. Add a SmartArt graphic to represent the hiring process to the email message.
   a) Place your cursor after the picture you inserted, and **Enter** twice to place two hard returns in the email message.
   b) Type *FYI, here is how we think the hiring process will take place:*
   c) Press **Enter** twice to place two hard returns in the email message.
   d) Select the **INSERT** tab and in the **Illustrations** command group, select **SmartArt**.
   e) In the **Choose a SmartArt Graphic** dialog box, select **Process** in the left **Navigation** pane.
   f) Select the second SmartArt graphic, **Step Up Process**.
   g) Select **OK** to insert the SmartArt graphic in the message body.
   h) Select the **[Text]** box in the first shape in the SmartArt graphic and type *Prescreen candidates*
   i) Select the **[Text]** box in the second shape in the SmartArt graphic and type *First-round interviews with HR*
   j) Select the **[Text]** box in the third shape in the SmartArt graphic and type *Second-round interviews with team*
   k) On the **SMARTART TOOLS** contextual tab, on the **DESIGN** tab, in the **Create Graphic** command group, select **Add Shape**. A new SmartArt shape is added to the process graphic.
   l) Type *Offer letters and hires!*

   > **Note:** You don't need to place your cursor in the new shape to type your text; it's already selected. Once the shape is added, type your text and it will appear in the graphic.

2. Apply a theme to your SmartArt graphic.
   a) Select the SmartArt graphic (if it is not already selected).
   b) On the ribbon, select the **OPTIONS** tab.
   c) In the **Themes** command group, select **Themes**.
   d) In the gallery, hover over the different types of themes, and view the preview of the theme applied to your SmartArt in the Live Preview.
   e) Select **Facet**. Verify that the SmartArt graphic has changed and the theme has been applied.

3. Select **Send** to send your enhanced message to the recruitment team.

4. View the message you sent in its entirety.
   a) In the **Folder** pane, select **Sent Items**.
   b) Select the email you just sent in the message list and view the email—with all of the text, formatting, attachments, and enhancements you included—in the **Reading** pane.
   c) In the **Folder** pane, select **Inbox** to return to your message list.

TOPIC F

Manage Automatic Message Content

You have composed a message and enhanced a message using the various graphical and text elements available in Outlook. Outlook also provides built-in features that allow you to create and implement automatic message content that appears in every email you send, such as signatures, stationery, and fonts. In this topic, you will manage automatic message content.

You can use graphical elements, themes, and styles to enhance your email messages as needed. But what about including other personal information that you might want to include in every email you send, like your name and contact information? Outlook is equipped with features that let you configure personalized message content like a signature, stationery, and other customized elements that are automatically included on all of your messages. Configuring this automatic message content ensures that your messages are personal and consistent every time you communicate via email.

Stationery and Themes

The **Stationery** feature provides design templates that you can apply to your HTML-formatted email messages in Outlook. Stationery templates include background colors or patterns that are displayed in the message body of your outgoing messages. Outlook provides a collection of these templates that you can use. You cannot create custom stationery.

There are also theme templates included in Outlook that can be applied to your HTML-formatted email messages. Similar to the themes that are applied to SmartArt and other message components, theme templates include a font and paragraph scheme, and background colors or graphics. You can manipulate theme templates to remove background colors or images and include vivid colors.

Stationery and themes can be selected as a default to be used for all of your new email messages, or you can apply them to a single message of your choice.

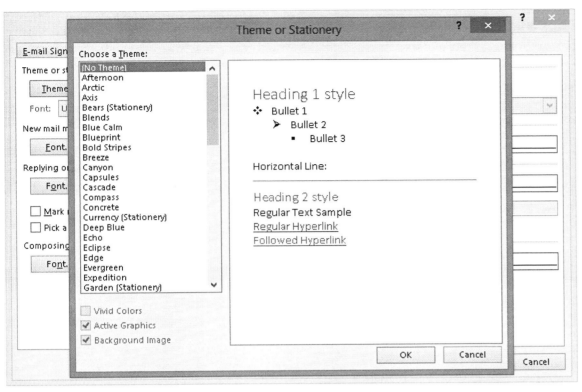

Figure 2-25: The Theme or Stationery dialog box displays the collection of stationery and themes available that can be applied to your HTML-formatted messages.

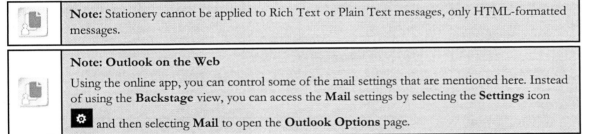

	Note: Stationery cannot be applied to Rich Text or Plain Text messages, only HTML-formatted messages.
	Note: Outlook on the Web Using the online app, you can control some of the mail settings that are mentioned here. Instead of using the **Backstage** view, you can access the **Mail** settings by selecting the **Settings** icon ⚙ and then selecting **Mail** to open the **Outlook Options** page.

	Access the Checklist tile on your CHOICE Course screen for reference information and job aids on How to Manage Personal Stationery Options.

Font Options

Outlook allows you to specify the fonts that will be used when sending, replying to, or forwarding HTML-formatted messages. There are even options to identify comments or change font colors in replies or forward. You can also determine which font will be used when interacting with plain text messages.

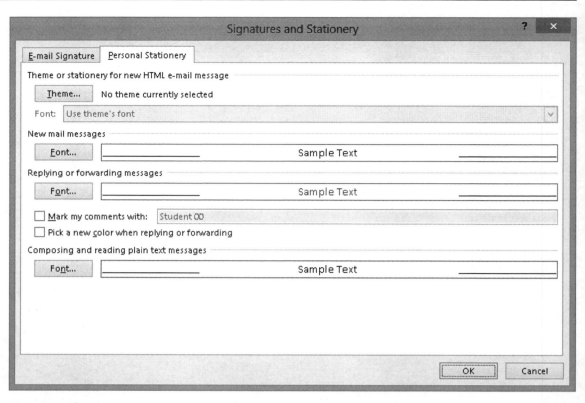

Figure 2-26: The Signatures and Stationery dialog box displays the font options for various types of messages.

Changing Font Colors For Multiple Responses In a Thread

To differentiate between multiple responses you have made to the same email thread, you can have Outlook automatically select a new font color for every new response in a thread. If you check the **Pick a new color when replying or forwarding** check box under **Replying or forwarding messages**, Outlook will apply a different font color to each of your responses (replies or forwards) within a specific thread. For that thread, the message content you enter in each response you make will appear in a different font color.

Note: Outlook on the Web

You can change the font and basic formatting that will be used in all messages. In other words, you cannot use different fonts for different types of messages.

Access the Checklist tile on your CHOICE Course screen for reference information and job aids on How to Specify Font Options.

ACTIVITY 2-7
Specifying Font Options

Scenario

You will be sending emails from your Develetech email account both internally within the organization and to external people that you communicate with often. You know that not all of the people you communicate with via email will be able to receive HTML-formatted messages. You want to specify the font options for the various message formats so that all of your recipients receive professional-looking emails from you.

---

1. Open the **Personal Stationery** dialog box where you will specify your font options.
   a) In the Outlook window, select **FILE→Options**.
   b) In the **Outlook Options** dialog box, select **Mail**.
   c) Select **Stationery and Fonts**. The **Signatures and Stationery** dialog box will open, with the **Personal Stationery** tab selected.

2. Specify the font option for new email messages.
   a) In the **New mail messages** section, select the **Font** button. [Font...] The **Font** dialog box opens.
   b) In the **Font** field, scroll down in the list to find and select **Lucida Sans Unicode**.
   c) In the **Font** style field, select **Regular**.
   d) In the **Size** field, select **10**.
   e) View what your font choices will look like in the **Preview** box.
   f) Select **OK** in the **Font** dialog box.

3. Specify the font option for replies or forwards.
   a) In the **Replying or forwarding messages** section, select the **Font** button. The **Font** dialog box opens.
   b) In the **Font** field, scroll down in the list to find and select **Lucida Sans Unicode**.
   c) In the **Font** style field, select **Regular**.
   d) In the **Size** field, select **10**.
   e) Select the **Font color** drop-down, and select **Blue, Accent 1, Darker 50%,** the fifth color from the left in the bottom row.
   f) View what your font choices will look like in the **Preview** box.
   g) Select **OK** in the **Font** dialog box.
   h) Check the **Mark my comments with** check box. In the text field, delete the default text and type your initials.

4. Specify the font options for plain text messages.
   a) In the **Composing and reading plain text messages** section, select the **Font** button. The **Font** dialog box opens.
   b) In the **Font** field, scroll up in the list to find and select **Arial**.
   c) The font style is automatically selected with the plain text default, **Regular**.
   d) In the **Size** field, select **10**.
   e) View what your font choices will look like in the **Preview** box.
   f) Select **OK** in the **Font** dialog box.

5. Save and apply the font options you specified.
   a) In the **Signatures and Stationery** dialog box, select **OK**.
   b) In the **Outlook Options** dialog box, select **OK**.

Signatures

A *signature* is a standard closing element that can be created, personalized, and then added to the end of your email messages. The signature identifies the sender of the email message, and usually includes the sender's name and contact information and possibly a picture, such as a company logo. A signature can also include hyperlinks that will open linked content, such as a link to a company website.

You can create multiple signatures that you can append to your email messages for different needs. You can append your signature to an email message manually, or you can configure the option to add your signature to your emails automatically.

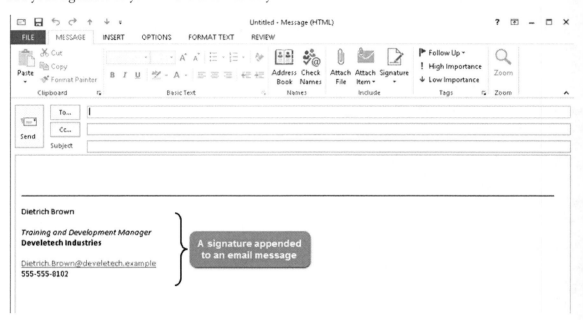

Figure 2-27: A signature appended to the end of an email message.

Note: Outlook on the Web

You have access to your email signature by opening the **Outlook Options** page from the **Settings** pane. From the **Options** list on the left, select **Mail→Layout→Email signature**. You have a variety of formatting options available and can also specify which types of messages you want the signature applied to.

Access the Checklist tile on your CHOICE Course screen for reference information and job aids on How to Manage Signatures For Messages.

ACTIVITY 2-8
Creating and Applying an Email Signature

Data File

C:\091043Data\Composing Messages\develetech_logo.png

Scenario

Now that Develetech is using Outlook as the email application for the organization, all employees have been instructed to create and apply a signature to their emails. Human Resources has asked that everyone create an email signature that includes some basic information about themselves such as their name, job title, and contact information and include the Develetech logo. Once you create your signature, you will need to apply it to your outgoing messages.

1. Create a new email signature.
   a) In the Outlook window, select **FILE→Options**.
   b) In the **Outlook Options** dialog box, select **Mail**.
   c) Select **Signatures**.
   d) In the **Signature and Stationery** dialog box, in the **Select signature to edit** section, select **New**.
   e) In the **New Signature** dialog box, type *Develetech* and select **OK**.

2. Compose and format your signature text.
   a) In the **Edit signature** section, place your cursor in the signature body.
   b) Type your first name and last name.
   c) Enter to insert a hard return.
   d) In the format bar, select the **Bold** button **B** type *Product Designer* and deselect the **Bold** button.
   e) Enter to insert a hard return and type your street address.
   f) Enter to insert a hard return and type your city, state, and zip code.
   g) Enter to insert a hard return and type your phone number.
   h) Select and highlight all the signature text you just typed, and from the **Font Type** drop-down, select **Garamond**.

3. Insert the Develetech logo at the bottom of your signature.
   a) Place your cursor at the end of your phone number, and press **Enter** twice to insert two hard returns.
   b) Select the **Picture** button. 🖼
   c) In the **Insert Picture** dialog box, navigate to the **C:\091043Data\Composing Messages** folder.
   d) Select **develetech_logo**.

    Note: You likely will not see the file extensions for your files. By default, they do not appear unless you have enabled them in the operating system. If you have enabled them, you would see the file as **develetech_logo.png**.

   e) Select **Insert**.

4. Apply the new signature to all your outgoing messages.
   a) In the **Choose default signature** section, in the **New messages** field drop-down, select **Develetech**.
   b) In the **Replies/forwards** field drop-down, select **Develetech**.
   c) Select **OK** in the **Signatures and Stationery** dialog box.
   d) Select **OK** in the **Outlook Options** dialog box.

5. Create a new email to view your signature.

   a) In the Outlook window, on the **HOME** tab, select **New Email** and verify that your signature appears in the message body.

   b) Close the message form.

Summary

In this lesson, you composed more sophisticated email messages using formatting, attachments, enhancements, and automatic content. Knowing how to use all of the features of Outlook that are available to you can help you compose more complex and professional email messages.

Which of the available Outlook features for composing and enhancing a message have you used in the past or do you think you would use in future email communications? Why?

What are some of your experiences with attaching files or items to your emails?

 Note: Check your CHOICE Course screen for opportunities to interact with your classmates, peers, and the larger CHOICE online community about the topics covered in this course or other topics you are interested in. From the Course screen you can also access available resources for a more continuous learning experience.

3 Reading and Responding to Messages

Lesson Time: 1 hour

Lesson Objectives

In this lesson, you will:

- Customize reading options.

- Work with attachments.

- Manage your message responses.

Lesson Introduction

Other than composing new emails to send to your recipients, reading and responding to emails that are sent to you are likely the other two actions that you will perform most often in Microsoft® Office Outlook®. In this lesson, you will read and respond to messages.

Simply opening and reading an email in Outlook is pretty simple. Responding to emails is a fairly easy and intuitive task. Even so, Outlook provides a number of features that make it easy to read and respond to the emails in your Inbox. Knowing how to take advantage of these features can help you address the emails in your Inbox in a timely and efficient manner.

TOPIC A

Customize Reading Options

You are familiar with the Outlook 2013 interface and how to navigate the application using the default settings. There are a number of options in Outlook that you can use to customize the way that can view and read emails in your message list. In this topic, you will customize these reading options.

Chances are, if you are using Outlook in a business organization, you will receive and read numerous emails every day. Opening and reading every email that comes into your inbox can be time consuming. Fortunately, you can customize your reading options in Outlook to help you maximize your time reading and responding to emails.

Desktop Alerts

Desktop alerts are notifications that appear on screen when a new Outlook item, such as an email message or meeting invitation, is delivered and arrives in your Inbox. When a new item is received, a small pop-up window will appear at the top right corner of your screen, on top of any open windows.

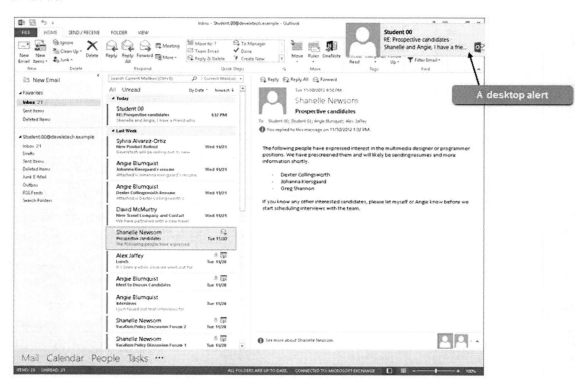

Figure 3-1: A desktop alert appears on-screen when a new Outlook item arrives.

Depending on the type of item received, the desktop alert will display varying information:

- For an email message, the desktop alert will display the sender, the subject line, and text from the first line in the message.
- For a meeting request, the desktop alert will display the sender, the subject line, and the date, time, and location of the meeting.
- For a task request, the desktop alert will display the sender, the subject line, and the start date for the task.

By default, desktop alerts are turned on, but you can turn off desktop alerts and all other forms of message arrival notifications if desired.

Other Message Arrival Notifications

There are other notifications that you can set to notify you when a new item arrives. These notifications include:

- Playing a sound.
- Briefly changing the appearance of the mouse pointer (if applicable).
- Showing an envelope in the taskbar until the email is marked as read.

Any combination of desktop alerts and notifications can be configured to best notify or remind you of new items in your Inbox.

Note: Outlook on the Web

When you receive new mail, a notification will appear in the upper-right corner of your browser window. Like the desktop alert in the desktop application, the notification box appears for a brief moment and you can select it to open the message in a separate browser window.

Pane Views

Views are options that you can use to control how data is displayed in Outlook. You can manipulate the views of the various panes that make up the Outlook window—the **Folder** pane, the **Content** pane, the **Reading** pane, and the **To-Do Bar**—to suit your personal preferences and make viewing your Outlook items easier. You can arrange the panes of the Outlook window with the commands available on the **VIEW** tab on the ribbon.

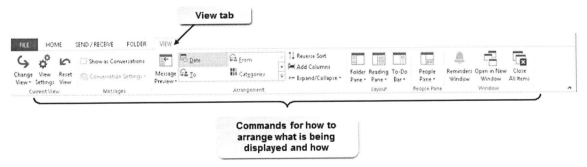

Figure 3-2: The VIEW tab provides commands for how to arrange what is being displayed in the Outlook window and how it is being displayed.

- The **Folder** pane can be minimized or turned off to provide more space for the **Content** pane and the **Reading** pane.
- By default, the **To-Do Bar** is turned off.
- The **Reading** pane can be docked either to the right of the **Content** pane or at the bottom of the **Content** pane, or it can be turned off altogether.
- The **Content** pane can be configured to display the items in various ways, including how items are arranged or sorted, which columns are displayed for items, and other advanced settings for the view selected.

Note: Outlook on the Web

To control the width of the **Folder** pane, you can simply drag the right border to the desired size. To change the display settings, you can select the **Settings** icon and then select **Display settings**. Using this link, you will have access to settings for the **Reading** pane, **Message list**, and **Conversations**. Select the desired category to make changes to those settings.

Message Preview

Message Preview is a feature in Outlook that displays the first few lines of a message in the **Content** pane, beneath the subject line of the message. Message Preview lets you read the beginning portion of the message to get a feeling for what the message is about, without having to open the message in the **Reading** pane or in a new Outlook window.

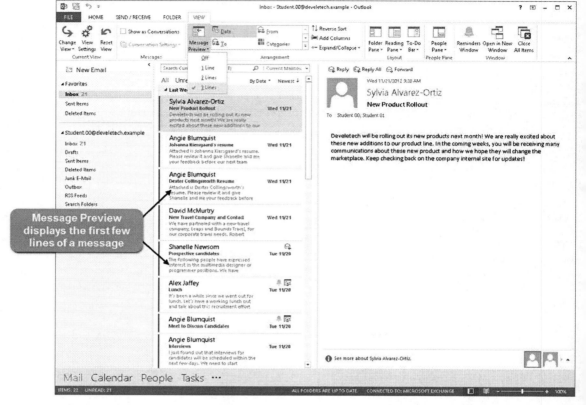

Figure 3-3: Message Preview can display up to three lines of text from the message body in the item in the message list.

By default, Message Preview is enabled, and displays one line of text from the message body. You can choose to modify the Message Preview to display up to three lines of text, or you can choose to disable the feature based on your personal preferences.

Conversations

Messages that you receive that are all part of the same thread of discussion and that share the same subject matter can be organized in Outlook using *conversations*. When conversations in Outlook are enabled, all messages that you have sent or received and which have the same subject line are grouped together with the subject line as the heading. When multiple messages are being sent back and forth between multiple people concerning the same subject matter, conversations can be a useful tool in organizing and managing these messages in your Inbox.

Conversations in your Inbox are identified with a right-pointing triangle ▷ at the far left of the most recent email message you have received that is part of the conversation thread. The entire message thread can be collapsed or expanded to hide or display all of the messages in the conversation thread. When a new email is received within the conversation, the entire conversation is moved to the top of your Inbox. If a conversation contains any unread messages, the most recent message in the conversation thread will display the colored bar to the left of the message and the blue, bold subject heading.

Note: Conversations can include messages across multiple folders in your Outlook environment. For instance, items you send are saved in your **Sent Items** folder, but when conversations are enabled, you will also see those items within the conversation. If you move messages that are part of a conversation to folders you have created within Outlook, while those messages will be saved and stored in that folder, they will also appear in your Inbox as part of that conversation.

Figure 3-4: A conversation displays multiple messages that have been sent and received regarding the same subject.

Split Conversations

A conversation can have more than one message thread within it; a conversation with multiple threads is called a split conversation. Split conversations may occur when someone replies to an earlier message rather than the latest message, forwards a message to a new recipient, or replies to only one person in a multiple-recipient thread.

Access the Checklist tile on your CHOICE Course screen for reference information and job aids on How to Customize Your Reading Options For Messages.

ACTIVITY 3–1
Customizing Your Reading Options

Scenario

Now that you have been working in the **Mail** workspace in Outlook for a little while, you have found that the default reading options do not suit your preferences. You want to customize your view of the **Mail** workspace and your reading options so that you can interact with the messages in your Inbox more quickly and efficiently.

---

1. Remove the **Favorites** section from displaying in the **Folder** pane.
   a) On the ribbon, select the **VIEW** tab.
   b) In the **Layout** command group, select **Folder Pane** and from the drop-down, deselect **Favorites**.

2. Change the location of the **Reading** pane.
   a) On the **VIEW** tab, select **Reading Pane**.

   Reading
   Pane ▾

   b) From the drop-down, select **Bottom**. Bottom

3. Change the columns that appear in the sort bar.
   a) On the **VIEW** tab on the ribbon, in the **Arrangement** command group, select **Add Columns**.

   📑 Add Columns

   b) In the **Show these columns in this order** box at the right, select **Size**.
   c) Select **Remove**. <- Remove
   d) In the **Show these columns in this order** box, select **Attachment**.
   e) Select **Move Down** twice to place the **Attachment** column between **Subject** and **Received**.
   Move Down
   f) Select **OK**.
   g) Verify that the columns in your sort bar have changed.

4. Change the arrangement of the items in your message list.
   a) In the **Arrangement** command group, select the **From** option.

   Arrangement

   b) Verify that the items in your message list are now sorted and arranged by the sender of the message in the **From** column.
   c) Select the **Date** option to sort and arrange you messages by the default of date received.

5. Configure the notifications you will receive when new items arrive in your Inbox.

    a) On the ribbon, select the **FILE→Options**.

    b) In the **Outlook Options** dialog box, select **Mail**.

    c) In the **Message arrival** section, uncheck the **Play a sound** check box and verify that **Briefly change the mouse pointer** check box is unchecked.

    d) Verify that the **Show an envelope icon in the taskbar** and **Display a Desktop Alert** check boxes are checked.

    e) Select **OK** in the **Outlook Options** dialog box.

TOPIC B

Work with Attachments

You have customized the way that you view and read the emails messages that you receive. If any of those messages include an attachment, you need to know how to work with the attached files to be able to read and respond to those emails in a timely manner as well. In this topic, you will work with attachments.

From time to time, you will receive an email that includes an attachment. Depending on the purpose of the attachment, you may just need to open and view the attached file, or you may need to save the attached file. Knowing how to work with attachments can help you manage the email messages in your Inbox.

Attachment Preview

The *attachment preview* feature in Outlook allows you to preview a file that has been attached to an email message in the **Reading** pane. With attachment preview, you can view and read attached files without having to open the message from the message list and without having to open the file in its associated application.

Figure 3-5: A preview of an attached file can be viewed in the Reading pane.

 Access the Checklist tile on your CHOICE Course screen for reference information and job aids on How to Work With Attachments.

ACTIVITY 3-2
Working With Attachments

Scenario

Since you are part of the recruitment team to hire new employees at Develetech, you have received quite a few emails in your Inbox that include attachments. Recently, most of those attachments have been the résumés of potential candidates. These attachments are starting to clutter up your Inbox and are taking up too much space in your Inbox. You want to print some of these attachments to review as hard copies, save some of the attachments to keep for future reference, and then remove some of the attachments to make more space in your Inbox.

1. Move the **Reading** pane to the right so you can preview an attachment more easily.
   a) On the ribbon, select the **VIEW** tab.
   b) Select **Reading Pane→Right**.

2. Preview an attachment in the **Reading** pane.
   a) In your message list in the Inbox, select the email from Angie Blumquist with the subject line "Dexter Collingsworth Resume."
   b) In the message content in the **Reading** pane, select the attached file **Dexter Collingsworth Resume.docx**.
   c) View the attachment in the **Reading** pane.

3. Print the attachment.
   a) Verify that the attachment is still selected in the message, and that the **ATTACHMENT TOOLS** contextual tab is visible.

    Note: If the tabs are not visible, select the attached file in the message body again to have them display.

   b) On the **ATTACHMENTS** tab, in the **Actions** command group, select **Quick Print**.

   Quick
   Print

   c) In the **Opening Mail Attachment** dialog box, select **Open**.
   d) The document will print to your default printer.

4. Save the attachment.
   a) Make sure that the attachment is still selected in the message body, and the **ATTACHMENT TOOLS** tab is still visible.
   b) On the **ATTACHMENTS** tab, in the **Actions** command group, select **Save As**.

   Save
   As

c) In the **Save Attachment** dialog box, in the left pane, select **Desktop**.

d) At the top of the dialog box, select **New folder**.

e) In the new folder title, type *Resumes* and press the **Enter** key.

f) Make sure the **Resumes** folder is selected.

g) Select **Open**.

h) Select **Save**.

5. Remove the attachment from the email message to free up space in your Inbox.

a) Make sure that the attachment is still selected in the message body, and the **ATTACHMENTS** tab is still visible.

b) On the **ATTACHMENTS** tab, in the **Actions** command group, select **Remove Attachment**.

X

Remove
Attachment

c) In the **Microsoft Outlook** dialog box, select **Remove Attachment**.

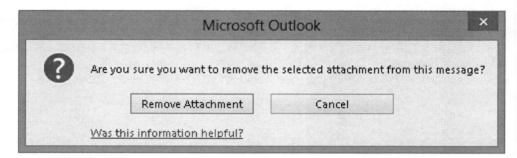

d) Observe that the attachment is no longer attached in the message.

TOPIC C

Manage Your Message Responses

You have customized the way you read and interact with messages, including those that include attachments. You also need to respond to the messages you receive. When you start responding to messages, you also have to manage your message responses. In this topic, you will manage your message responses.

Often, you are using email to communicate important information. You want to make sure that your emails are sent successfully, read in a timely manner, and include all the information you need to convey. You can use the features available in Outlook—such as voting, tracking, resending and recalling—to help you manage your message responses.

 Access the Checklist tile on your CHOICE Course screen for reference information and job aids on How to Configure Message Response Options.

The InfoBar

The InfoBar is a banner that appears near the top of an open or selected Outlook item, below the ribbon in an open item and below the subject and sender in the **Reading** pane view, and provides information about the item.

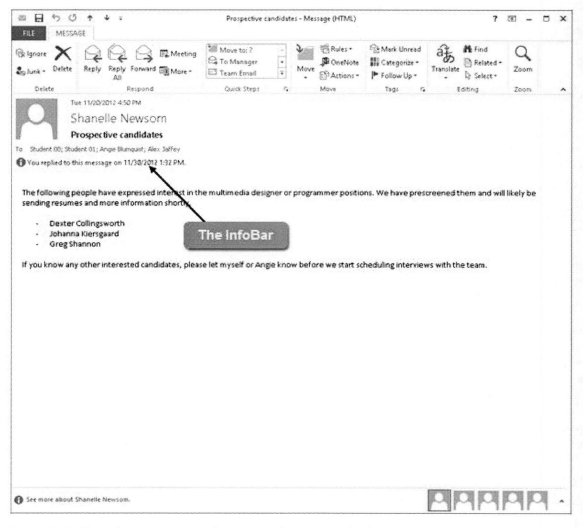

Figure 3-6: The InfoBar provides information about an Outlook item.

Depending on the type of item, the InfoBar may display:

- The date and time you replied to or forwarded an email.
- If a message has been flagged for follow-up.
- If a message has been categorized with a color category.
- The date and time you responded to a meeting invite, and how you responded (accepted, denied, tentatively accepted, and more).
- Other information about the item, such as if extra line breaks were removed from a message.

Voting and Tracking Options

You can use the voting and tracking options provided in Outlook to follow the actions taken on emails you send, whether a new message or a reply message. These options are found in the **Tracking** command group on the **OPTIONS** tab of the message form.

☐ Request a Delivery Receipt

Use Voting   ☐ Request a Read Receipt
Buttons ▾

Tracking   ⌞ₐ

Figure 3-7: The voting and tracking options in Outlook.

The **Use Voting Buttons** option lets you send an email to your recipients that includes a simple poll. The answer options include **Approve;Reject, Yes;No, Yes;No;Maybe,** or a custom response you created. When voting options have been included in an email, the InfoBar displays text telling the recipients to vote; recipients then select and send their choice via an email response. The results can be tracked in the sender's message list.

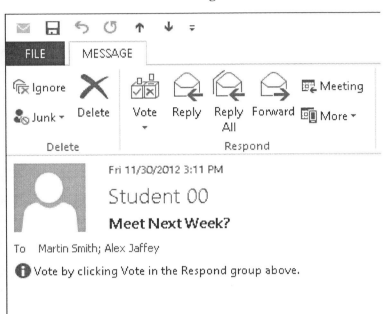

Figure 3-8: When voting options have been enabled, text will appear in the InfoBar of the message that instructs recipients to send their vote via the Respond group.

	Note: Outlook on the Web
	Using the online app, you can receive messages with voting buttons and use them to cast a vote; however, you cannot add voting buttons to a message from within the online app. To do so, you need to use the desktop application.

The **Request a Delivery Receipt** option can be enabled for an email to keep track of when the email was delivered. If this option is enabled, you will receive a message from Microsoft Outlook notifying you that your message was delivered successfully.

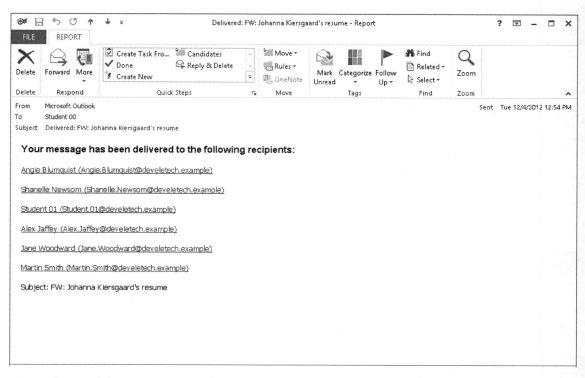

Figure 3-9: A delivery receipt notifies you that your email has been delivered.

The **Request a Read Receipt** option can be enabled for an email to keep track of if and when your email was read by the intended recipient. If this option is enabled, you will receive a message from the recipient notifying you that your message was read.

 Note: When you enable read receipts, the recipient is notified that you have requested a read receipt for the email. The recipient can choose whether or not to send the confirmation notification. They can also choose to ignore all read receipts requested of them.

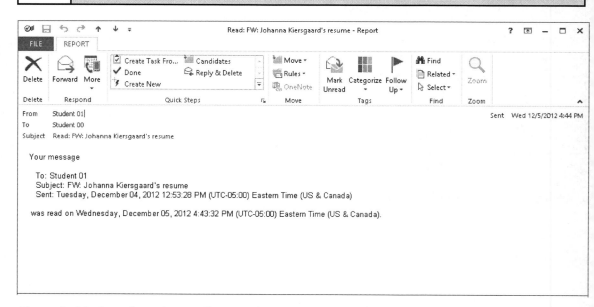

Figure 3-10: A read receipt notifies you that your recipient has read your email.

Note: Outlook on the Web

You can request delivery receipts and read receipts to messages by selecting **More commands→Show message options** to open the **Message options** dialog box. You can also set the **Sensitivity** of the message in this same dialog box.

Note: For more information about using the read receipt option to track an email, check out the LearnTO **Track an Email Using Read Receipts** presentation from the **LearnTO** tile on the CHOICE Course screen.

Access the Checklist tile on your CHOICE Course screen for reference information and job aids on How to Use Voting and Tracking Options.

ACTIVITY 3-3
Using Tracking Options

Scenario

You need to forward an earlier email from Angie Blumquist to the rest of the recruitment team. Your message is very important and includes information that you need to make sure the team receives. You want to make that it will be delivered successfully, so you want to use the tracking options in Outlook to be notified that it has been.

1. Forward the email about Johanna Kiersgaard's résumé to the recruitment team.

   a) In the message list, select the message from Angie Blumquist with the subject line "Johanna Kiersgaard Resume."

   b) On the **HOME** tab on the ribbon, select **Forward**.

   Forward

   c) In the message in the **Reading** pane, select **Pop Out**.

   d) In the message form, address the email message to Alex Jaffey, Jane Woodward, and Martin Smith.

   e) Copy Angie Blumquist and Shanelle Newsom on the message.

   f) In the message body, type *Johanna Kiersgaard will be coming in for an interview this afternoon. Please review her resume (attached) ASAP and join us at 2 p.m. in Conference Room B.*

    Note: Remember that you do not have to type this text verbatim, and you can type other text if it is appropriate.

2. Enable tracking options for your email message.

   a) On the ribbon, select the **OPTIONS** tab.

   b) In the **Tracking** command group, check the **Request a Delivery Receipt** check box.

   ☐ Request a Delivery Receipt

3. Select **Send** to send the message with your tracking option enabled.

4. Verify that you receive your tracking notifications.

   a) In the **Quick Access Toolbar** at the top left of the screen, select **Send/Receive All Folders** to refresh your message list.

   b) Verify that you receive a message from Microsoft Outlook with the subject line "Delivered: FW: Johanna Kiersgaard Resume."

    Note: It may take a few minutes to receive the delivery receipt, depending on how quickly the Microsoft® Exchange Server® can process and send the notification.

The Resend Option

There may be times when you need or want to resend a message that you have already sent. Perhaps you forgot to include a recipient or need to add a recipient, or received a tracking notification that your message was not successfully sent. The resend option in Outlook allows you to resend your email messages easily and quickly.

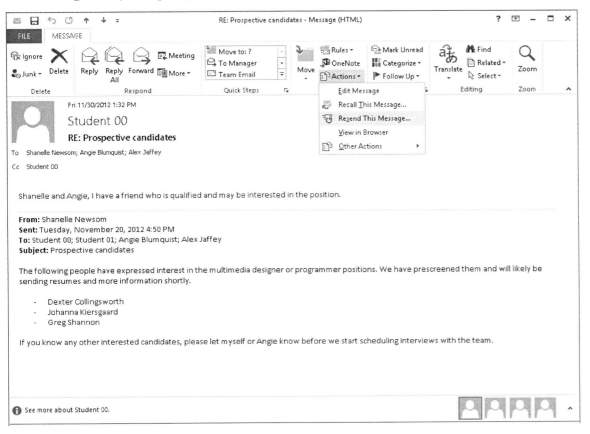

Figure 3-11: The resend option is available for sent messages in Outlook.

 Note: Outlook on the Web

The advanced message options to resend or recall messages are only available in Outlook 2013.

The Recall Option

There may be times when you need or want to recall a message that you have already sent. Perhaps you sent a message to the wrong person, sent the message too soon and need to revise the information, or forgot to attach a file. If the message has not yet been read by any of your recipients, you can use the recall option in Outlook to stop the delivery of your message altogether or, if desired, stop the delivery of the message and replace it with a new message.

 Note: The recall option is only available when Outlook is being used with Exchange Server, and only for emails sent to Exchange Server accounts. You will not be able to recall messages that you sent to email addresses outside of your organization or using other email clients.

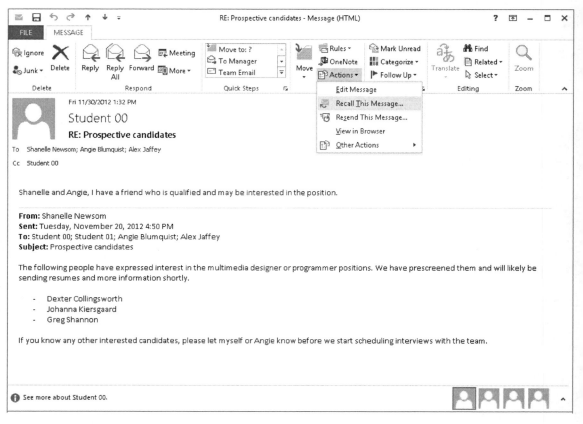

Figure 3-12: The recall option is available for messages sent between Exchange accounts in Outlook.

 Note: Both the resend and recall options are only available if you save and store your sent items. By default, a copy of items you send is stored in your **Sent Items** folder. You can customize if your sent items are saved at all, and where these items are saved. You can choose to have all sent items saved to a different folder, or select where specific messages will be saved (i.e. to a specific folder) on a message-by-message basis using the **Save Sent Item To** command on the **Options** tab in the message form for an unsent message.

 Access the Checklist tile on your CHOICE Course screen for reference information and job aids on How to Resend or Recall Messages.

ACTIVITY 3-4
Recalling a Sent Message

Data File

Dexter Collingsworth Resume.docx

Scenario

You are sending numerous emails to the recruitment team, and sometimes you send them with mistakes and without including all the information. You send an email to the team and forget to include the time that an interview candidate is coming in to talk. You want to recall the message before the team reads the message, and replace the message with one that includes the interview time.

1. Send the original message to the recruitment team.
   a) Create a new email message.
   b) Address the email message to Alex Jaffey, Jane Woodward, and Martin Smith.
   c) Give the message the subject line *Dexter Collingsworth Interview*
   d) In the message body, type *Dexter Collingsworth will be coming for an interview today.*
   e) Select **Send** to send the message.

2. Recall the message and replace it with a new message that has been fixed.
   a) In the **Folder** pane, select the **Sent Items** folder.
   b) In the message list, select and open the message you just sent with the subject "Dexter Collingsworth Interview."
   c) On the ribbon, in the **Move** command group, select **Actions→Recall This Message**.

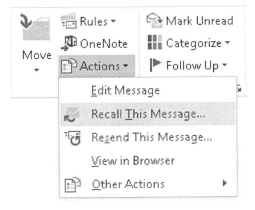

    d) Select the **Delete unread copies and replace with a new message** radio button.

    e) Verify that the **Tell me if recall succeeds or fails for each recipient** check box is checked.

    f) Select **OK**. Your original message form will open.

    g) In the message body, after the first line of text, type *Dexter will be joining us in Conference Room C at 3 p.m. this afternoon.*

    h) Select **Send**.

3. Close the original Dexter Collingsworth Interview message.

4. In the **Folder** pane, select **Inbox** to return to your message list.

Summary

In this lesson, you used the available options in Outlook for reading and responding to messages. Knowing how to customize your reading options, work with attached files, and use features available in Outlook to manage your responses will help you read and respond to your messages and items more quickly and efficiently.

Do you utilize the options for customizing your Reading view in Outlook, or do you use the default views? If you have customized the reading options, how has it helped you organize and manage your emails in your message list?

Do you currently use any of the features or options available in Outlook to help you manage your responses, such as voting, tracking, recalling, or resending? What are your experiences with these available features?

 Note: Check your CHOICE Course screen for opportunities to interact with your classmates, peers, and the larger CHOICE online community about the topics covered in this course or other topics you are interested in. From the Course screen you can also access available resources for a more continuous learning experience.

4 Managing Your Messages

Lesson Time: 40 minutes

Lesson Objectives

In this lesson, you will:

- Manage messages using tags, flags, and commands.

- Organize messages using folders.

Lesson Introduction

You have sent and received email messages. As the volume of messages in your Inbox increases, you may find it more difficult to read, respond to, and manage the space in your Inbox. In this lesson, you will manage your messages.

As you start to use Microsoft® Office Outlook® more and more, you may receive many messages and your Inbox may become unwieldy. You may need to find emails you have received and responded to quickly, or you may need to use visible reminders to identify emails that require your response. By using the features available in Outlook to organize and manage your emails, you can rest assured that the emails that need your attention are being attended to in a timely and professional manner.

TOPIC A

Manage Messages Using Tags, Flags, and Commands

You have composed, read, and responded to Outlook items. It will be far easier to make sure that you are attending to the items that need your attention if you can identify them visually. In this topic, you will use tags, flags, and commands in Outlook to manage your email messages.

Once you start using Outlook to send and reply to emails, your Inbox and folders will quickly fill up with messages and items that need your attention. How will you know which needs your attention most: which messages you need to read, which need you to respond or complete a task, and which you can ignore? You can use the tags, flags, and commands provided in Outlook to help you manage and organize your messages before they clutter your Inbox, and you can't handle the volume.

Mark as Unread/Read

When a message or item arrives in your Inbox, it is indicated as a new message and one that has not been read yet using the blue bar on the left of the message, and blue, bold font for the subject line text. You can use the **Unread/Read** command, found in the **Tags** command group on the **HOME** tab on the ribbon, to help keep track of the items in your Inbox. Even if you didn't read an item, or read it in the **Reading** pane, you can mark it as read to identify to yourself that it has been handled. Or, oppositely, even if you have already read an email but you want to make sure you come back to the item, you can mark it as unread to give yourself a visual reminder that you need to respond to the item.

Figure 4-1: The Unread/Read command in the Tags command group lets you change the read status of items in your message list.

Color Categories

You can categorize your Outlook items using *color categories*, which are color codes that you can customize and assign to items in your Inbox and other folders. You can customize a color category with a specific color and name, and then assign that category to messages, contacts, appointments, and other items to associate them using the category title. Assigning a color category to your items helps you to quickly identify items in your folders and track your interactions with those items.

Note: To see the color categories that have been applied to items, you must have the **Categories** field displayed in the message list. If it is not displayed, you can display the column by selecting the **VIEW** tab on the ribbon, selecting **Add Columns** in the **Arrangement** command group, and adding the column to your sort bar or moving the field to a location where you can see it. A small box with the color code you selected will display in the **Categories** field for that item.

Color categories can be customized and assigned to items using the **Categorize** command in the **Tags** command on the ribbon.

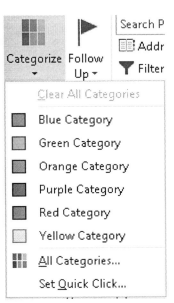

Figure 4-2: The Categorize command allows you to select a color category to assign to your items.

Color Categories and Conversations

A color category that is applied to the top-level message within a conversation thread will be applied to all current and future messages and threads in the conversation. When you attempt to assign a color category to the original item within a conversation thread, Outlook will notify you that this color category will be applied to all items that are part of the selected conversation.

Quick Click for Color Categories

If there is one color category that you frequently use to categorize items in your message list, you can select this color category to be used as your Quick Click for categories. You can select the category using **Categorize→Set Quick Click**. When you select the **Categories** icon for an item in your message list (if the field is displayed in your **Content** pane), the item is tagged with the color code associated with that category.

Shortcut Keys

When you set up a color category, you can also configure a shortcut key to apply to that category. A shortcut key will allow you to use a combination of keystrokes that you configure, such as **Ctrl + F2,** to categorize an email or item with that color category without having to select it from the **Categorize** command group.

Note: Outlook on the Web

You can create and apply color categories to your messages, but if you want to change the categories options, such as the assigned shortcut key, you must use Outlook 2013.

Access the Checklist tile on your CHOICE Course screen for reference information and job aids on How to Use Tags to Manage Your Messages.

ACTIVITY 4-1
Using Tags to Manage Messages

Scenario

The recruitment effort to hire new employees at Develetech that you are a part of is really picking up. Numerous emails, meeting invites for interviews, and attached résumés are being sent to and from the recruitment team. Your Inbox is starting to become full, and you are having a hard time keeping track of the emails you have received. You want to use tags to help you visually manage the items in your Inbox.

1. Create a custom color category for your emails regarding the recruitment effort.

   a) In the message list in the **Content** pane, find and select the email message from Shanelle Newsom with the subject line "We're Hiring!"

    Note: When you create a new color category, it is automatically applied to whichever item you have selected in your message list. It is recommended that you first select an email that you want to apply this new color category to before you create the new color category.

   b) On the **HOME** tab on the ribbon, in the **Tags** command group, select **Categorize**.

   Categorize

   c) From the gallery, select **All Categories**.

   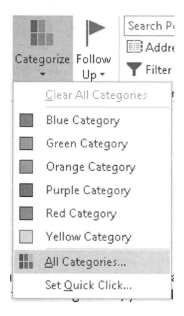

   d) In the **Color Categories** dialog box, select **New**.

   e) In the **Add New Category** dialog box, in the **Name** field, type *Recruitment*

f) From the **Color** drop-down, select the **Dark Orange** color option.

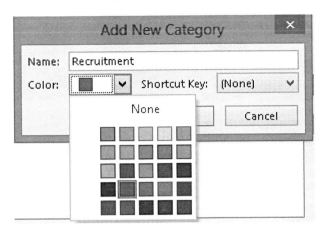

g) From the **Shortcut Key** drop-down, select **CTRL+F11**.

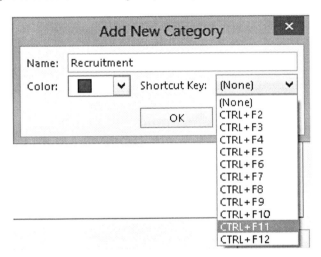

h) Select **OK** in the **Add New Category** dialog box.
i) Select **OK** in the **Color Categories** dialog box.
j) Verify in the message list that the We're Hiring! email now displays a dark orange box in the **Categories** column for the message and that a dark orange bar titled "Recruitment" displays in the InfoBar in the **Reading** pane view of the message.

2. Categorize other emails regarding the recruitment effort with the **Recruitment** color category you created.
   a) In the message list, find and select the email from Angie Blumquist with the subject line "Job description for review?"
   b) On the **HOME** tab on the ribbon, in the **Tags** command group, select **Categorize**.

c) From the **Categorize** gallery, select **Recruitment**.

d) In the message list, find and select the email message from Angie Blumquist with the subject line "Recruitment and Interviews."

e) In the message list, also find and select the email from Angie Blumquist with the subject line "Interviews."

 Note: If applicable, use **Ctrl+Click** to select multiple messages at once.

f) On your keyboard, press **Ctrl** and **F11** simultaneously to use the shortcut key to apply the **Recruitment** category to the selected emails.

 Note: If you are using a technology that does not allow you to use shortcut keys, select the **Recruitment** category from the **Categorize** gallery instead.

g) In the message list, find and select the email from Shanelle Newsom with the subject line "Prospective Candidates."

h) Select the **Recruitment** category for the message using the method of your choice.

Flag for Follow-Up

Outlook allows you to use follow-up flags to mark certain messages in your folders for follow-up actions. Using the **Follow Up** command in the **Tags** command group on the ribbon, you can mark messages and items and set a reminder to yourself to perform an action on the item at a later date. When you flag a message, the message will display the **Follow up** flag icon.

 Note: If the **Tasks** component of the **To-Do Bar** has been enabled, a follow up reminder for the task will display there as well.

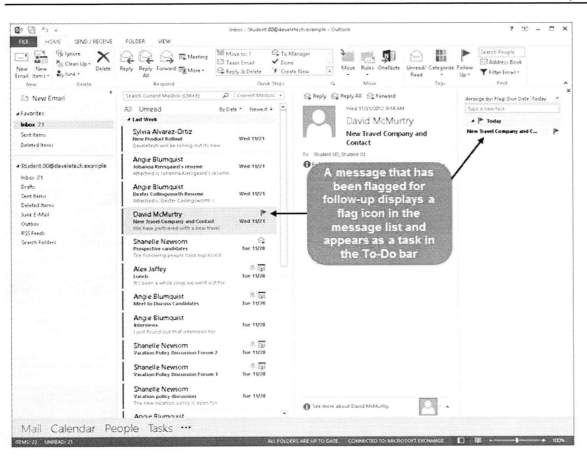

Figure 4-3: A message flagged for follow-up.

Follow-Up Flag Options

There are a number of options you can choose from when you flag an item for follow-up. These options are available when you select an item and select the **Follow Up** command on the ribbon.

Flag Option	Description
Today	Flags the item with a start date and due date of the current day. The default reminder is an hour before the end of workday time established in Outlook.
Tomorrow	Flags the item with a start date and due date of the next day. The default reminder is the start of the following work day.
This Week	Flags the item with a start date of two days from the current day, and a due date no later than the last day of the work week. The default reminder is the start of the work day on the start date (the beginning of the work day two days from the current day).
Next Week	Flags the item with a start date of the first work day of the following week and a due date of the last work day of the following week. The default reminder is the start of the work day of the following week.
No Date	Flags the item without a start date or end date. There is no reminder for this flag.
Custom	Flags the item with a start date and due date of your choosing. You choose what to do as your follow-up action, select a start date and due date, and set up a reminder for the follow-up action.

Flag Option	Description
Add Reminder	Allows you to specify a reminder date and time that is different from the default reminder for the flag type you selected. You can also choose a different reminder sound.
Mark Complete	Marks the flagged item as complete. A completed flagged item is indicated with a **Checkmark** icon in the **Flag Status** field in the message list.
Clear Flag	Removes the follow-up flag and all reminders for this item.

Set Quick Click for Flags

If there is one flag type that you frequently use to mark your items for follow-up actions, you can select this flag type to be used as your Quick Click for flags. You can select the Quick Flag type using **Follow Up→Set Quick Click**. When you select the **Flag Status** icon for an item in your message list (if the field is displayed in your Content pane), the item is flagged for follow-up with the Quick Flag type.

Note: Outlook on the Web

Flags work the same way in the online app. If you want to create a custom flag, add a reminder, or use the **Quick Click** feature, you must use Outlook 2013.

Access the Checklist tile on your CHOICE Course screen for reference information and job aids on How to Use Flags to Manage Your Messages.

ACTIVITY 4-2
Using Flags to Manage Messages

Scenario

David McMurtry recently sent a message that included contact information for your new corporate travel representative. You know that you will need to make travel arrangements for an upcoming trip to a convention, and you want to be sure that you save the contact information. You are too busy at the moment to do so, so you want to flag the email for follow-up to deal with it tomorrow when you have more time.

Flag David's message for follow-up.

a) In the message list, find and select the email message from David McMurtry with the subject line "New Travel Company and Contact."

b) On the **HOME** tab on the ribbon, in the **Tags** command group, select **Follow Up**.

Follow
Up ▾

c) Select **Custom**.

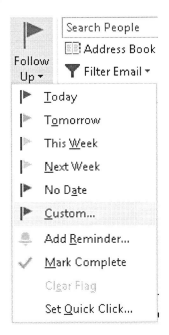

d) In the **Custom** dialog box, verify that the **Flag to** field is automatically populated with **Follow up**.

e) Select the **Start date** field drop-down, and in the calendar, select the following business day.
f) Select the **Due date** field drop-down, and in the calendar select two business days from the current date.
g) Check the **Reminder** check box.
h) From the date drop-down, select the following business day.
i) From the time drop-down, select **9:00 AM**.
j) Select **OK** in the **Custom** dialog box to flag the selected message.
k) Verify that the message now displays a flag in the **Flag Status** column in the message list.

The Ignore Conversation Command

Messages and replies that you receive as part of a message thread can clutter your Inbox. Perhaps you were included on the original message as a recipient, and replies keep coming to you from the other recipients who use the **Reply All** option, even though you don't need to be included on the responses. The **Ignore Conversation** command in Outlook allows you to ignore new messages that you receive as part of a message thread that you no longer want to be a part of. When you use the **Ignore Conversation** command, all messages within the message thread that are currently in your Inbox and any future messages you receive as part of the message thread are automatically moved into the **Deleted Items** folder.

Message threads that you have chosen to ignore using the **Ignore Conversation** command can be recovered and restored to your Inbox from the **Deleted Items** folder.

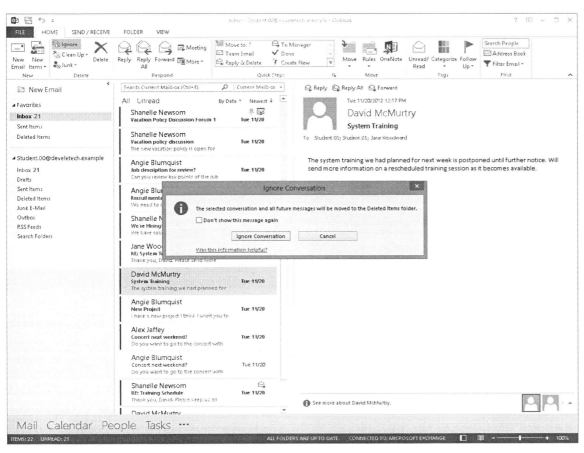

Figure 4–4: The Ignore Conversation command moves all current and future messages in a conversation thread to the Deleted Items folder.

Note: Outlook on the Web

The **Sweep** feature serves a similar purpose in the online app. When you select the **Sweep** command, you can choose from the following four options:

- Delete all messages from the selected sender.
- Delete all, including future messages.
- Always keep the latest message and delete the rest.
- Always delete messages older than 10 days.

Clean Up Commands

The **Clean Up** commands helps prevent clutter and open up space in your Inbox and other folders by detecting and eliminating redundant messages that are part of message threads. The **Clean Up** commands evaluate the contents of the messages in a thread for redundancy. If the contents of one message are completely contained within another, the previous iterations of that message are cleaned up and moved to the **Deleted Items** folder (by default) or a folder you create.

There are three **Clean Up** commands that can be applied:

- **Clean Up Conversation** evaluates and removes redundant messages only within the message thread of a message that is selected in the message list.
- **Clean Up Folder** evaluates and removes redundant messages from every message thread within the selected folder.
- **Clean Up Folder & Subfolders** evaluates and removes redundant messages from every message thread within the selected folder and any of its subfolders.

Figure 4-5: The Clean Up commands evaluate and remove redundant messages in your conversations.

	Note: Outlook on the Web The **Clean Up** commands are not available in the online app.

	Access the Checklist tile on your CHOICE Course screen for reference information and job aids on How to Use Commands to Manage Your Messages.

ACTIVITY 4-3
Using Commands to Manage Messages

Scenario

On any given day, you receive many emails in your Inbox. Sometimes, those emails are important and you need to keep track of them, like you did with tags and flags. Other emails aren't as important for you: sometimes you are copied on responses that don't really pertain to you, or emails pile up in your Inbox that are all part of one conversation that could be consolidated. You want to use the **Ignore Conversation** and **Clean Up** commands to help manage your email messages. You will use the **Ignore Conversation** command to ignore a conversation about system training on which you were originally included as a recipient of and no longer need to be a part of. And you will use the **Clean Up** command to consolidate the message threads in a conversation about the training schedule include only the latest and most comprehensive message.

---

1. Ignore the email thread about the system training, which you do not need to be a part of.

   a) In the message list, find and select the email message from Jane Woodward with the subject line "RE: System Training."

   b) On the **HOME** tab on the ribbon, in the **Delete** command group, select **Ignore**. 🔳 Ignore

   c) In the **Ignore Conversation** dialog box, select **Ignore Conversation**.

   d) In the **Folder** pane, select **Deleted Items**.

   e) Verify that the original message from David McMurtry with the subject line "System Training" and the response message from Jane Woodward with the subject line "RE: System Training" have been moved to the **Deleted Items** folder.

   f) Select one of the ignored messages, and verify that on the **HOME** tab of the ribbon in the **Delete** command group, the **Ignore** button is now highlighted, indicating that the message has been ignored successfully.

2. Clean up the message thread about the training schedule to include only the latest and most comprehensive message.

   a) In the **Folder** pane, select **Inbox**.

   b) In the message list, find and select any of the messages with the subject line "Training Schedule?"

c) On the **HOME** tab on the ribbon, in the **Delete** command group, select **Clean Up** and select **Clean Up Conversation**.

d) In the **Clean Up Conversation** dialog box, review the warning message and select **Clean Up**.

e) In the message list, verify that the only message left with the subject line "Training Schedule?" is from Shanelle Newsom.

f) Select or open this email message and scroll through the entire message body to verify that it includes all of the messages pertaining to the training schedule, including the original email and all responses in the message thread.

g) In the **Folder** pane, select **Deleted Items**.

h) Verify that the original message from Jane Woodward with the subject line **Training Schedule?** and the response message from David McMurtry with the subject line **RE: Training Schedule?** have been moved to the **Deleted Items** folder.

i) In the **Folder** pane, select **Inbox** to return to the message list.

TOPIC B

Organize Messages Using Folders

You managed your messages using tags, flags, and other commands in Outlook. It will be even easier to find, interact with, and store messages if you organize them into different and specialized locations. In this topic, you will organize your messages and items using folders.

Using visual prompts and other features in Outlook like tags can help you manage your interactions with the emails in your Inbox. It will be even easier to manage your Outlook items if you keep them organized in folders. In Outlook, you can create and use folders to store messages and items that all relate to one specific subject, such as a project. With folders, you can quickly and easily locate all the items you need to respond to or follow-up on in one location.

Default Email Folders

Every Outlook 2013 installation includes a number of default email folders that have been created and are available for you to use right away to store your email messages. These default email folders are available for all of your email accounts, if you are accessing more than one account profile through one Outlook instance. These default email folders include:

- **Inbox**
- **Drafts**
- **Sent Items**
- **Deleted Items**
- **Junk E-mail**
- **Outbox**
- **RSS Feeds**
- **Search Folders**

Default email folders in Outlook cannot be moved, renamed, or deleted.

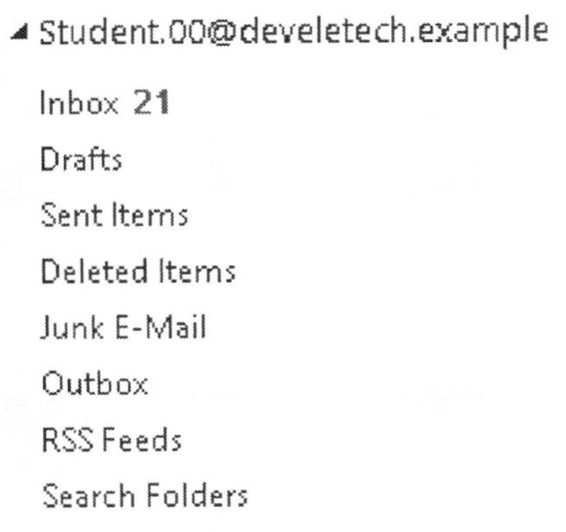

▲ Student.00@develetech.example

  Inbox **21**

  Drafts

  Sent Items

  Deleted Items

  Junk E-Mail

  Outbox

  RSS Feeds

  Search Folders

Figure 4-6: The default email folders are included with every Outlook install and are immediately available to store your messages.

Note: Outlook on the Web

In addition to the default folders in Outlook 2013, the online app also includes a **Notes** folder and a **Clutter** folder. The **Notes** folder is specific to the online app and replaces the **Notes** view that appears in the desktop application. The **Clutter** feature can only be activated from within the online app and is covered in more detail in the *Microsoft® Office Outlook® 2013: Part 2* course.

Note: The default Outlook folder **Sent Items** is also the default location where your sent items are saved, but you can customize where and how your sent items are saved. For more information, check out the LearnTO **Customize Where and How Sent Items Are Saved** presentation from the **LearnTO** tile on the CHOICE Course screen.

Email Folders on the Server

You can create new folders in addition to the default email folders provided in Outlook to help your store and organize your messages. You can use these folders to store and save emails that are all related to a specific subject, such as a project.

Folders you create are saved on the Exchange Server and utilize storage space that has been allocated to you for your Inbox. The amount of space allocated to you is determined by your system administrator.

Folders you create on the server are added to your folder list in the **Folder** pane.

Note: Folders you create do not inherit the **Reading** view or layout that you have customized for your Inbox. You either need to manually customize the reading options and layout for each folder, or use the **Apply Current View to Other Mail Folders** option, found in the **Change View** command on the **VIEW** tab.

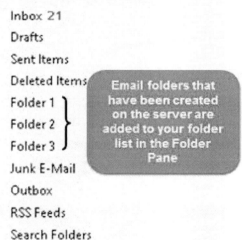

Figure 4-7: Email folders created on the server.

Personal Folders

You can also create *personal folders* in Outlook to organize and store your messages and items, especially those you may want to keep private. Personal folders are saved as personal store table (.pst) files and are stored on the local computer, rather than the Exchange Server. Because these folders are stored locally, personal folders are available whether or not you are connected to the Exchange Server network and do not utilize the storage space allocated for your Inbox.

 Access the Checklist tile on your CHOICE Course screen for reference information and job aids on How to Organize Messages Using Folders.

ACTIVITY 4-4
Organizing Messages Using Folders

Scenario

When you start sending and receiving messages in large quantities, your Inbox can quickly become difficult to manage. An easy way to organize and keep track of the messages and items you receive is to create and use folders to store related messages. You want to create a parent "Recruitment" folder where eventually all the information about your recruitment efforts will be stored. Then, you will create a "Candidates" subfolder, where you will store the emails you have received about the potential candidates for the open positions.

---

1. Create a **Recruitment** folder on the server at the same level as your default folders.
   a) Select the **FOLDER** tab on the ribbon.
   b) In the **New** command group, select **New Folder**. The **Create New Folder** dialog box appears.
   c) In the **Name** field, type *Recruitment*
   d) In the **Select where to place this folder** section, select the top level, which is your email account.

   e) Select **OK** in the **Create New Folder** dialog box.

f) In the **Folder** pane, verify that the **Recruitment** folder was created, and is now located between the default folders **Outbox** and **RSS Feeds**.

> Inbox
> Drafts
> Sent Items
> Deleted Items
> Junk E-Mail
> Outbox
> **Recruitment**
> RSS Feeds
> Search Folders

2. Create a **Candidates** subfolder within the **Recruitment** folder.

   a) On the **FOLDER** tab on the ribbon, in the **New** command group, select **New Folder**. The **Create New Folder** dialog box appears.

   b) In the **Name** field, type *Candidates*

   c) In the **Select where to place this folder** section, select the **Recruitment** folder you created.

   d) Select **OK** in the **Create New Folder** dialog box.

   e) In the **Folder** pane, verify that the **Candidates** folder was created and is now located as a subfolder underneath the **Recruitment** folder.

> Inbox
> Drafts
> Sent Items
> Deleted Items
> Junk E-Mail
> Outbox
> ◢ Recruitment
>   **Candidates**
> RSS Feeds
> Search Folders

3. Move the messages related to potential candidates to the **Candidates** folder you created.

   a) In the **Folder** pane, select **Inbox**.

   b) In the message list, find and select the email message from Shanelle Newsom with the subject line **Prospective Candidates**.

   c) On the **HOME** tab on the ribbon, in the **Move** command group, select **Move**.

   d) From the list of available folders in the **Move** drop-down list, select **Candidates**.

   e) In the message list, find and select the email message from Angie Blumquist with the subject line "Dexter Collingsworth Resume."

   f) In the **Move** command group, select **Move→Candidates**.

   g) In the message list, find and select the email message from Angie Blumquist with the subject line Johanna Kiersgaard Resume and drag it into the **Candidates** folder.

   h) In the **Folder** pane, select the **Candidates** folder and verify that the messages now appear in the message list for the folder.

4. Copy the messages from the **Candidates** folder and place copies in the **Recruitment** folder.
   a) Select all the messages in the message list in the **Candidates** folder.
   b) In the **Move** command group, select **Move→Copy to Folder**.
   c) In the **Copy Items** dialog box, select **Recruitment**.
   d) Select **OK**.
   e) In the **Folder** pane, select the **Recruitment** folder and verify that the messages now appear in the message list for the folder.

5. In the **Folder** pane, select **Inbox** to return to the message list.

Summary

In this lesson, you used the available features in Outlook for managing your messages and items. Using these available features will help you manage your messages and items: using visual cues such as color categories and flags to keep track of your items; using commands to keep your Inbox tidy and uncluttered; and using folders to organize your items.

How do you currently manage your email messages? How would you use the options available in Outlook to help you manage your messages?

Do you think that you would use any of the command options that are provided in Outlook? How and why?

 Note: Check your CHOICE Course screen for opportunities to interact with your classmates, peers, and the larger CHOICE online community about the topics covered in this course or other topics you are interested in. From the Course screen you can also access available resources for a more continuous learning experience.

5 Managing Your Calendar

Lesson Time: 1 hour, 5 minutes

Lesson Objectives

In this lesson, you will:

- View the calendar.
- Manage appointments.
- Manage meetings.
- Print your calendar.

Lesson Introduction

You have managed your email messages in Microsoft® Office Outlook® 2013. Outlook also provides a robust calendar environment where you can keep track of your own personal appointments and schedule and meetings with other Outlook users. In this lesson, you will manage your calendar.

With Outlook 2013, not only can you use email messages as a form of communication, you can also use the calendar environment to communicate and interact with other users. Using the calendar feature in Outlook, you can schedule and manage meetings with other people and organization resources, or use appointments to keep track of your own personal events.

TOPIC A

View the Calendar

So far, you have mostly worked in the Outlook **Mail** workspace, familiarizing yourself with and using the email functionality to manage your email communications. You can also use the **Calendar** workspace to view any upcoming events you have scheduled. In this topic, you will view the calendar.

You will likely use Outlook primarily to manage your email communications. But there are many other features available in Outlook to help you manage your time and interactions with other people, such as the **Calendar**. Getting to know the **Calendar** workspace and how to use it to manage your upcoming events can help manage both your own time and your time spent interacting with others.

Types of Calendar Entries

There are three main types of calendar entries in Outlook: appointments, meetings, and events. An *appointment* is an activity that you can schedule at a specific time in your calendar and does not require inviting other people or using other resources such as an online meeting or conference room. A *meeting* is an activity which requires inviting other people and possibly requires utilizing other resources available in Outlook. An *event* is an all-day instance of an appointment or a meeting.

Appointments, meetings, and events can all be scheduled as a one-time instance, or they can be made to recur multiple times, during the same timeslot, and for a specific purpose.

Recurring events are indicated in your calendar with the recurrence symbol.

 Note: Outlook on the Web

Using the online app, you can create, view, and edit your Outlook calendar events using procedures that are similar to the ones used in the desktop application. To view your calendar events, select the **App Launcher** icon and then select the **Calendar** tile. The **Calendar** page is a simplified version of the desktop calendar.

Calendar Grid Arrangement Options

You can choose to arrange and view the calendar grid in any of the different configurations found in the **Arrangement** command group on the **VIEW** tab.

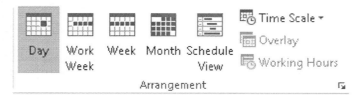

Figure 5-1: The Arrangement commands on the View tab modify the arrangement of the calendar grid.

Options include:
- **Day** displays the schedule of all calendar entries for a specific date, broken down into hourly timeslots.
- **Work Week** displays the five days of a typical work week (Monday through Friday), and the schedule of all calendar entries on those days, broken into hourly timeslots.

- **Week** displays all days in the week (Sunday through Saturday), and the schedule of all calendar entries on those days, broken into hourly timeslots.
- **Month** displays the entire month selected and the schedule of all calendar entries on each day of that month, but does not display the timeslots for each entry.
- **Schedule View** displays a detailed schedule for the current date and time, broken into hourly timeslots for the remainder of the time left in the current day.

Note: Outlook on the Web

There are four different calendar views that you can choose from: **Day, Work Week, Week,** and **Month** views. You can select the desired view from the options in the upper-right corner of the window. Your agenda for the selected day appears along the right side of the window. This is similar to the **Schedule View**, and you can select the double chevrons to hide or show it, as desired.

Time Scale Options

Each hourly timeslot is, by default, divided up into 30-minute segments. Using the **Time Scale** command in the **Arrangement** group, you can select a different increment to divide up each hourly timeslot. The smaller the time scale is in minutes, the more space is available to include details about the specific calendar entry.

Note: The **Time Scale** cannot be modified for the **Month** arrangement option.

The **Time Scale** options include:

- **60 Minutes**
- **30 Minutes**
- **15 Minutes**
- **10 Minutes**
- **6 Minutes**
- **5 Minutes**

The Weather Bar

The Weather bar—located at the top of the calendar grid in the Content pane, below the ribbon—displays the weather information for the next three days for a selected city. By default, the location that displays in the Weather bar will be the city that corresponds to the market version of Outlook that you have installed, for instance New York, NY.

You can customize the Weather bar to suit your preferences, including selecting whether the Weather bar displays, changing or adding locations, and configuring other options such as whether information is displayed in Fahrenheit or Celsius.

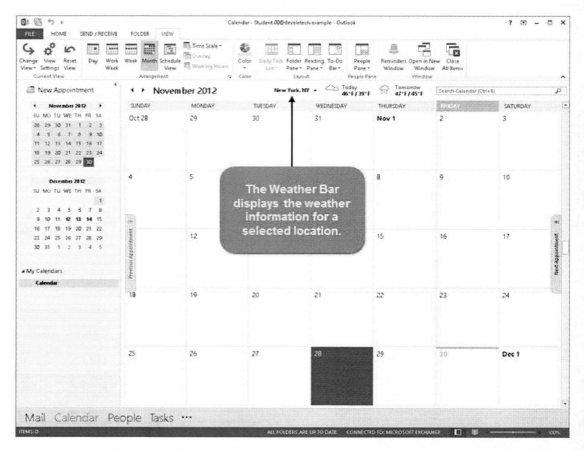

Figure 5-2: The Weather bar displays the weather information for a selected location above the calendar grid in the Content pane.

	Note: Outlook on the Web In the online app, a weather icon appears for each day of the current week. The location of the weather icon depends on the calendar view that is selected; however, it is consistently located near the day or date. You can select the weather icon to display a pop-up window with weather details, such as the temperature and a link to the complete forecast at **foreca.com**. If you have multiple locations, you can use the arrows in the upper-right corner of the pop-up window to scroll through the additional locations.

The Daily Task List

The **Daily Task List** is an optional pane in the **Calendar** workspace that appears in the calendar grid. The **Daily Task List** displays any tasks that you have scheduled in the **Tasks** pane. By default, the **Daily Task List** is off, but can be configured to display at the bottom of the calendar grid, below your schedule.

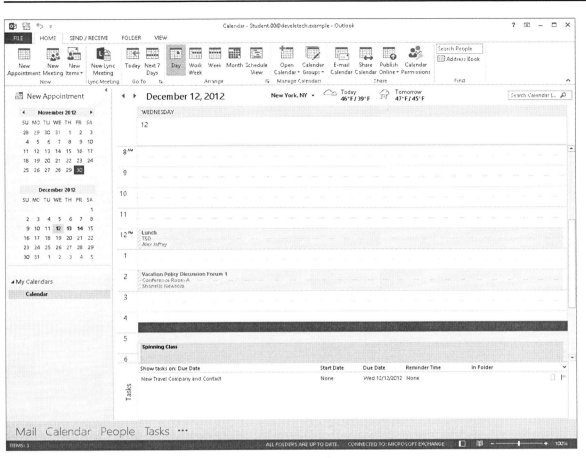

Figure 5-3: The Daily Task List displays any scheduled tasks in the Tasks pane at the bottom of the calendar grid.

 Note: Outlook on the Web

The Daily Task List and the calendar layout options are not available in the online app.

Calendar Layout Options

You can customize the layout of the **Calendar** workspace by modifying which components display and how, including the **Daily Task List,** the **Folder** pane, the **Reading** pane and the **To-Do Bar**. These options can be modified in the **Layout** command group on the **VIEW** tab.

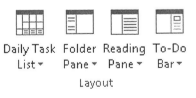

Figure 5-4: The Layout commands let you customize the Calendar workspace by modifying which components are displayed and how.

By default, the **Folder** pane is displayed normally at the left side of the screen, and both the **Reading** pane and the **To-Do Bar** are turned off and do not display.

The **Daily Task List** can only be displayed and modified when the **Day, Work Week,** or **Week** arrangement has been selected.

 Access the Checklist tile on your CHOICE Course screen for reference information and job aids on How to Customize Your Calendar Views.

ACTIVITY 5-1
Customizing Your Calendar View

Scenario

Your company, Develetech, recently implemented Outlook as the organization's email client. One of the reasons Outlook was selected was to implement the use of the calendar throughout the organization. You will be using the calendar often to schedule your own personal appointments and meetings, and to keep track of where you and your colleagues are throughout the day. It is important to customize the calendar view in a way that can help you best manipulate and manage your calendar entries.

1. On the **Navigation** bar, select **Calendar** to open your Outlook **Calendar** workspace.

Mail Calendar People Tasks •••

2. Explore the Weather bar.
   a) View the weather information that appears in the Weather bar for your default location.
   b) Select the down-arrow next to the current location and select **Add Location**.
   c) In the search box, type *Sante Fe* and select **Search**.
   d) In the list of search results, select **Santa Fe, NM**.
   e) Verify that the location in the Weather bar changes and now displays the weather information for Sante Fe, New Mexico.
   f) Toggle between the weather information for Santa Fe, NM and your default location using the down-arrow next to the location.

3. Explore the different calendar **Arrangement** options.
   a) On the ribbon, select the **VIEW** tab.
   b) Verify that the default **Month** option is selected in the **Arrangement** pane.
   c) View that the **Content** pane displays the calendar for the entire month in the calendar grid, with today's date highlighted.
   d) In the **Arrangement** command group, select **Day**.
   e) View that the **Content** pane displays the calendar for today's date only.
   f) In the **Arrangement** command group, select **Work Week**.
   g) View how only the five work days in the current work week are displayed in the calendar in the **Content** pane.
   h) Select **Week**.
   i) View how all the days in the current week, including the weekends, are displayed in the calendar.
   j) Select **Time Scale**.
   k) From the drop-down, select **15 Minutes** and view how the time grid displayed at the left of the calendar changes to 15-minute increments.
   l) Select **Time Scale** again and select **60 Minutes** and view how the time grid at the left changes to one-hour increments.

4. Select **Work Week** and **Time Scale** of **30 minutes** to be your arrangement view.

5. Explore the different calendar **Layout** options.
   a) On the **VIEW** tab on the ribbon, in the **Layout** command group, select **Daily Task List**.

b) Verify that the default view for the **Daily Task List, Off** is selected and that the **Tasks** pane does not display in the calendar grid.

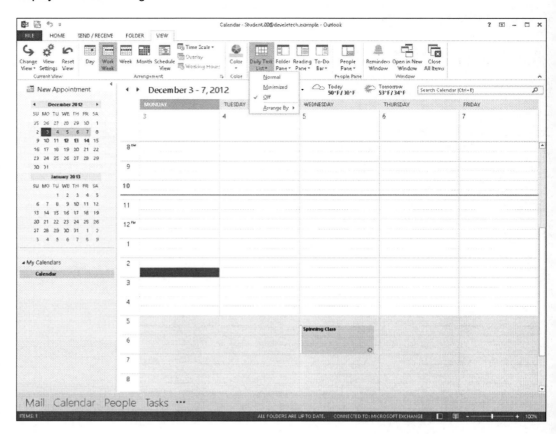

c) From the list of **Daily Task List** options, select **Normal** and verify that the **Tasks** pane appears at the bottom of the screen below the calendar grid.

d) In the **Layout** command group, select **Folder Pane**.

e) Verify that the default option **Normal** is selected and that the **Folder** pane is displayed at the left of the screen.

f) From the list of **Folder Pane** options, select **Minimized** and verify that the **Folder** pane to the left of the calendar grid is now minimized.

g) In the **Layout** command group, select **Reading Pane** and verify that the default option **Off** is selected and the **Reading** pane is hidden.

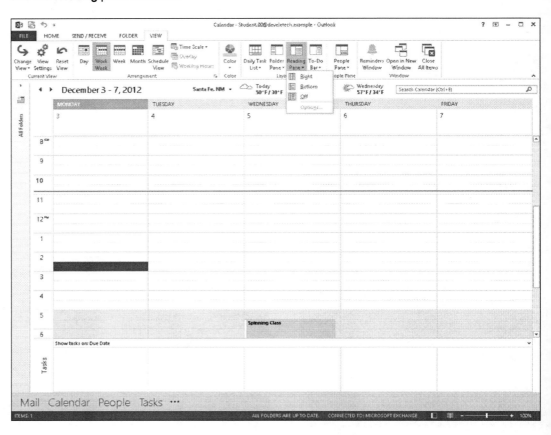

h) From the list of **Reading Pane** options, select **Right** and verify that the **Reading** pane is now displayed to the right of the calendar grid.

i) In the calendar grid, find and select the calendar entry titled **Lunch**.
j) View the details for the lunch meeting in the **Reading** pane at the right of the calendar grid.

k) Select the **VIEW** tab, select **To-Do Bar**, select **People** and verify that the **To-Do Bar** now appears at the far right of the screen, displaying the **Favorites** component.

l) Select the **Expand the Folder** pane arrow at the top of the minimized **Folder** pane [>] to display the **Folder** pane again.

m) Examine how your calendar appears now that all components of the calendar layout are displaying on screen.

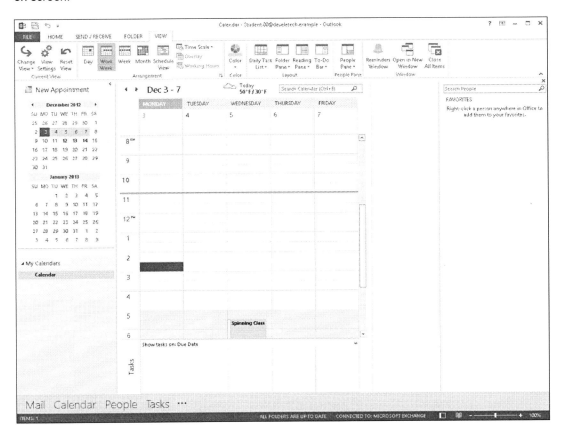

n) Minimize the Daily Task List, turn off the **Reading** pane, and close the People component of the To-Do Bar to return the calendar to a view where the calendar grid is the focus.

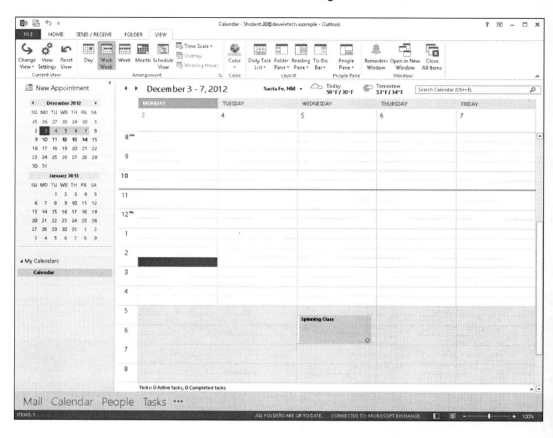

TOPIC B

Manage Appointments

Now that you are familiar with the **Calendar** workspace and how to view the events you create and manage within the calendar, you can start working with those events. Using the calendar to schedule appointments will be helpful to keep track of your own personal events and keep your calendar up-to-date for your colleagues to know your availability. In this topic, you will manage appointments.

It is important that you use the calendar in Outlook to keep track of your own individual time during working hours. This includes scheduling and managing your personal events using the appointments feature. Using appointments, you can keep track of the time that you are unavailable or out of the office, both to help remind you of these personal events and to make your colleagues aware of your availability or whereabouts.

The Appointment Form

Appointments are scheduled in Outlook using the **Appointment** form. When you select **New Appointment** from the **New** command group, a blank **Appointment** form opens.

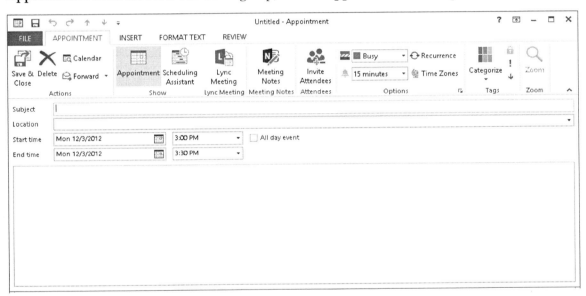

Figure 5–5: Details and options for an appointment are entered into an Appointment form.

The **Appointment** form has a number of fields where you enter the details and information about your appointment and select any necessary options to schedule the appointment on the calendar.

- In the **Subject** field, you enter a brief description or subject matter of the appointment.
- In the **Location** field, you enter the location where the appointment is occurring.
- In the **Start time** field, you select the date when the appointment begins from the calendar and a start time from the drop-down.
- In the **End time** field, you select the date when the appointment ends from the calendar and an end time from the drop-down.
- If the appointment is an all day event, with no specific time, check the **All day event** check box.
- In the message body, you can enter any specific information about the appointment.

Note: Outlook on the Web

In the online app, all three types of calendar entries are created by using the same command of **New→Calendar event**.

Reminders

Reminders are visual and auditory alerts that you can set for your calendar entries to notify you in advance of an upcoming event. The default reminder for all day events is 18 hours prior to the event; the default reminder for events with specific times are 15 minutes prior to the event. You can select different reminder times or choose to have no reminder at all for appointments or meetings you create.

Reminders can be selected from the **Reminder** drop-down in the **Options** command group of a new event form.

Figure 5-6: Reminders can be selected from the Reminder drop-down in the Options command group in any new event form.

 Note: Outlook on the Web

In addition to setting a reminder alert with sound, you can also send an email reminder to the attendees or just yourself.

Show As Options

The **Show As** options, found in the **Options** command group of an appointment or meeting form, can be used to indicate your availability status during a scheduled calendar entry to other people looking at your calendar. Marking your calendar entries with a **Show As** option can help accurately reflect your availability to those looking to schedule meetings with you or to know your whereabouts.

Figure 5-7: The Show As options indicate your availability status for specific times on your calendar.

The show options include:

- **Free** indicates you are available during that time period.
- **Working Elsewhere** indicates that you are working offsite.
- **Tentative** indicates that you may be available during that time period.

- **Busy** indicates that you are busy during the scheduled time period.
- **Out of Office** indicates that you will neither be available nor in the office during the scheduled time period.

Note: Outlook on the Web
You can specify the **Show As** and **Private** options directly in the new calendar event form.

The Private Option

If you have included information for a personal calendar entry that you want to see as a reminder to yourself, but do not want to make it visible to anyone able to view your calendar, you can mark the entry as **Private**. When you mark calendar entries as **Private,** other people can see that you are unavailable during the scheduled time but cannot view the specific details of the appointment, such as the subject or message body. The **Private** option is found in the **Tags** command group on the main tab of a new event form.

Private calendar entries are indicated in your own calendar with the lock symbol 🔒 displayed in the lower-right corner of the calendar entry.

Note: If you have delegated access rights or have granted read permissions for your calendar to other people, they will be able to view your calendar entries and see the details of your entries, unless you mark them **Private**.

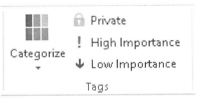

Figure 5-8: The Private command in the Tags command group.

Access the Checklist tile on your CHOICE Course screen for reference information and job aids on How to Manage Appointments.

ACTIVITY 5-2
Creating an Appointment

Scenario

Since Develetech will be using the Outlook calendar to keep track of people's availabilities and schedule meetings around those availabilities, it is important that your calendar accurately reflects your day-to-day schedule. You want to schedule and manage appointments for yourself in your calendar, for a variety of reasons: to help you keep track of your own personal appointments and to allow your colleagues to view your availability and schedule meetings with you accordingly.

You have a doctor's appointment the following Monday morning at 8:30, and you want to make a personal appointment for it in your calendar. Since you want to use the appointment to remind yourself as well, you want to make the appointment private so your colleagues can see that you are unavailable, but cannot see the details of the appointment.

---

1. Create the appointment for your doctor's appointment on your calendar.

   a) In the calendar grid, select the **Forward** arrow in the date view to move the calendar to the following week.

   b) In the calendar grid, select the **8:30 a.m.** time slot on Monday.

   c) If necessary, select the **HOME** tab on the ribbon.

   d) In the **New** command group, select **New Appointment**.

   > Note: You can also double-click on a calendar time slot bring up the **New Appointment** form.

   e) In the blank appointment form, in the **Subject** field, type *Dr. Burnett's*

   f) In the **Location** field, type *Atlas Office Park*

   g) Verify that the **Start time** field displays the date of the following Monday and **8:30 AM**.

   h) In the **End time** drop-down, select **9:30 AM (1 hour)**.

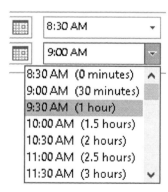

i) In the **Options** command group, select the **Show As** drop-down and select **Out of Office**.

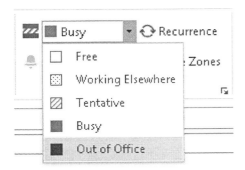

j) In the **Options** command group, select the **Reminder** drop-down and select **None**.

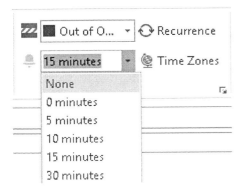

2. In the **Tags** command group, select the **Private** lock icon to make the appointment private.

3. Give your doctor's appointment a color category to visually differentiate it on your calendar.

a) In the **Tags** command group, select **Categorize**.

Categorize

b) Select **Blue Category**.
c) In the **Rename Category** dialog box, in the **Name** field, type **Personal** and select **Yes**.

d) Verify that the **Personal** color category appears in the InfoBar, above the subject line, in the appointment form.

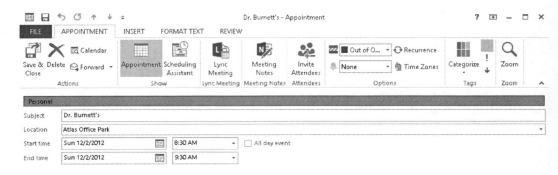

4. Select **Save & Close** to save the doctor's appointment to your calendar.

TOPIC C

Manage Meetings

Now that you have managed appointments in the calendar to keep track of time for your own personal events, you can begin to use the calendar to schedule and manage events that involve your coworkers and your organization's resources. Using the calendar to schedule and manage meetings can help you manage your time and the time you spend with others. In this topic, you will manage meetings.

More than likely, you will mainly be using Outlook to manage your email communications with your coworkers and colleagues. But you can also take advantage of the **Calendar** feature in Outlook to schedule, track, and manage meetings quickly and easily with your coworkers and using your organization's available resources, like conference rooms. Knowing how to use the **Calendar** workspace to manage your meetings will help you and your coworkers best organize your time efficiently.

The Meeting Scheduling Process

There is a fairly standard process that takes place to schedule meetings in the **Calendar** workspace in Outlook:

1. The meeting organizer sends a meeting request to recipients that have been identified as participants.
2. The meeting is automatically entered on the meeting organizer's calendar when sent.
3. Recipients respond to the meeting request in the manner appropriate to their availability during the meeting time.
4. If accepted, the meeting is automatically entered on each recipient's calendar.
5. A message is sent to the meeting organizer with the response from each recipient.

 Note: Outlook on the Web

Scheduling meetings works the same way in the online app. Within the calendar event form, you have buttons and drop-down menus to specify meeting details, find a room, and use the **Scheduling Assistant** feature.

The Meeting Form

Meetings are scheduled in Outlook using the **Meeting** form. When you select **New Meeting** from the **New** command group, a blank **Meeting** form opens.

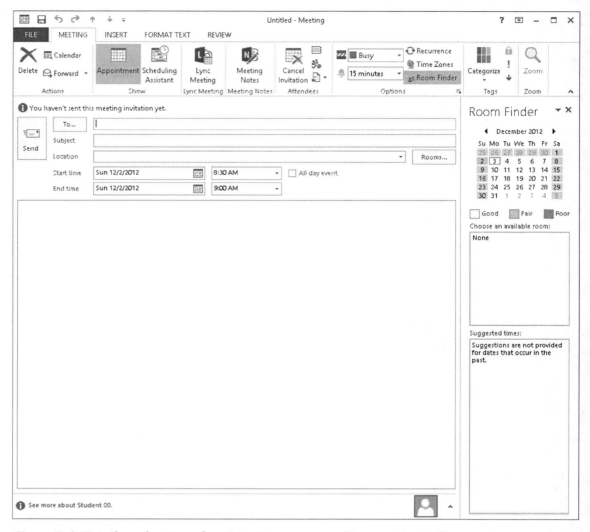

Figure 5-9: Details and options for a meeting are entered into a meeting form.

The **Meeting** form has a number of fields where you enter the details and information about your meeting, select your attendees, and select the necessary options to schedule the meeting.

- In the **To** field, you select your attendees.
- In the **Subject** field, you enter a brief description or subject matter of the meeting.
- In the **Location** field, you can enter the location where the meeting is occurring or select **Rooms** to find and select a room that has been designated as a shared resource for the organization, such as a conference room.
- If the appointment is an all-day event, with no specific time, check the **All day event** check box.
- In the **Start time** field, you select the date when the meeting begins from the calendar and a start time from the drop-down.
- In the **End time** field, you select the date when the meeting ends from the calendar and an end time from the drop-down.
- In the message body, you can enter any specific information about the appointment.

Meeting Reminders

You can also set reminders for meetings. The meeting organizer sets the reminder for the meeting when they send the meeting request, but it can be changed by the recipients to suit their own personal preferences once they have accepted the invite. The default reminder for new meetings is 10 minutes prior to the event.

Resource Booking Attendant

The **Resource Booking Attendant** automates the process of accepting or declining meeting requests regarding shared resources, like conference rooms. This feature works by setting policies for automating the meeting response. Policies can be set to book each individual resource.

 Note: While you will typically follow the process of using the **New Appointment** or **New Meeting** commands to schedule new events, you can also do so directly from an email message. For more information, check out the LearnTO **Schedule an Appointment or Meeting from an Email Message** presentation from the **LearnTO** tile on the CHOICE Course screen.

The Room Finder Pane

The **Room Finder** pane helps you select the best time and location for your meeting. Based on the recipients, date, and time that you have selected in the **Meeting** form for your meeting, the **Room Finder** pane displays important information about the availability of these resources:

- At the top of the pane is a calendar, which displays the date you have selected.
- Below the calendar, the **Choose an available room** section displays the rooms that are available during the time frame you have selected on the date you have selected.
- At the bottom of the pane, the **Suggested times** section displays any conflicts that may occur for any of the intended attendees for the date and time selected. It also suggests times for your meeting when most, if not all, of your attendees are available.

If the **Room Finder** pane does not appear in your **Meeting** form, on the **MEETING** tab, in the **Options** command group, select **Room Finder**.

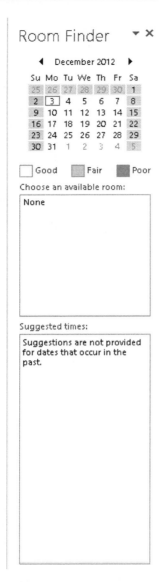

Figure 5-10: The Room Finder pane opens in the Meeting form and helps you find an available room for a meeting.

The Scheduling Assistant

The **Scheduling Assistant** is another tool available in a **Meeting** form that helps you identify the availability of participants and resources you are including on a meeting request. The **Scheduling Assistant** can be found on the **MEETING** tab, in the **Show** command group. Once you have added the date, time, and required attendees and resources to your meeting form, you can open the **Scheduling Assistant** to view any possible conflicts for the meeting time, view your attendees availabilities for other time frames, and select the best time for the meeting.

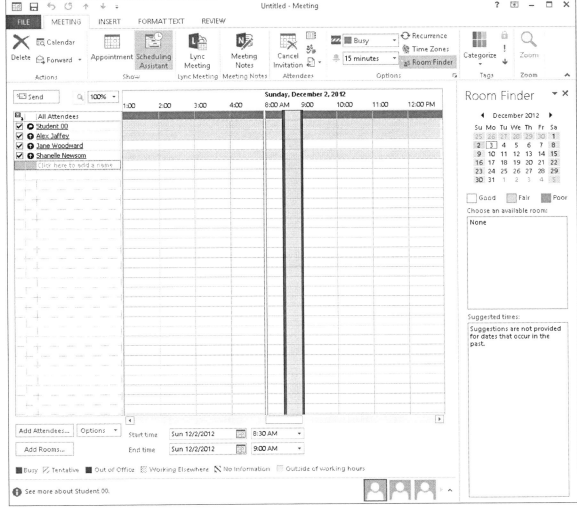

Figure 5-11: The Scheduling Assistant helps you identify the availability of your participants and resources for a specific meeting request.

 Note: When you open the **Scheduling Assistant,** the **Room Finder** pane is automatically opened as well.

Toggle Between Meeting Form Views Using the Show Commands

You can toggle between the **Appointment** and **Scheduling Assistant** commands, found in the **Show** command group on the **MEETING** tab in a **Meeting** form, to change the view of the meeting form. If you have opened the **Scheduling Assistant,** you can return to the message form to continue to add information to the meeting request by selecting **Appointment**.

Share Meeting Notes Using OneNote

One of the most common things that participants in a meeting actually do during the meeting is take notes. Outlook 2013 offers a way to share the notes that you and others take during a meeting with one another, using other Office 2013 products. Outlook 2013 integrates seamlessly with OneNote 2013 to help you easily share the notes you have taken during a meeting with the other attendees on the meeting invite. You can share your notes using OneNote before your meeting by integrating a link with OneNote in the meeting request, or during a meeting by sharing your OneNote document with the meeting attendees.

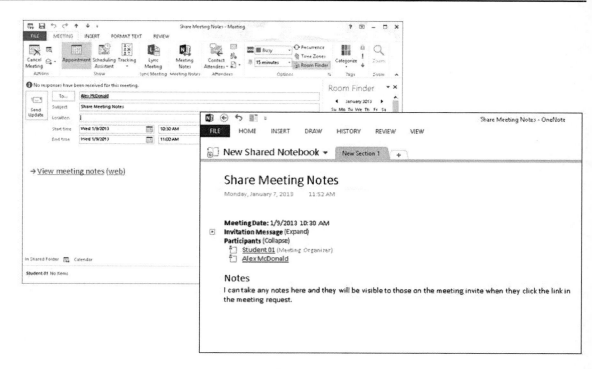

Figure 5-12: When meeting notes are shared using OneNote, a link to the OneNote document is placed in the meeting request, and the meeting information is placed in the linked OneNote document.

 Note: Outlook on the Web

Incorporating OneNote meeting notes into an Outlook meeting is not available when using Outlook on the web. However, you can share your OneNote notes with others by sharing from within OneNote directly and not through Outlook.

Meeting Response Options

There are a number of response options available for responding to a meeting request.

Response Option	Description
✓ Accept	Use **Accept** to accept the meeting invitation and place the meeting on your calendar. You can choose to accept and send a response to the meeting organizer, accept and not send a response to the meeting organizer, or accept and edit the response to include information in a message to the meeting organizer.
？ Tentative	Use **Tentative** to tentatively accept the meeting invitation and place the meeting on your calendar. You can choose to tentatively accept and send a response to the meeting organizer, tentatively accept and not send a response to the meeting organizer, or tentatively accept and edit the response to include information in a message to the meeting organizer. The **Tentative** response would most likely be used in situations when you are not a required attendee or to indicate that you may be able to attend the meeting.

Response Option	Description
Decline ▼	Use **Decline** to decline the meeting invitation. You can choose to decline and send a response to the meeting organizer, decline and not send a response to the meeting organizer, or decline and edit the response to include information in a message to the meeting organizer.
Propose New Time ▼	Use **Propose New Time** if you cannot attend the meeting at the time scheduled. You can either tentatively accept the meeting and propose a new time, or decline the meeting and propose a new time. If you do not choose either option (**Tentative** or **Decline**), and simply choose **Propose New Time,** by default you tentatively accept the meeting. The meeting is placed on your calendar at the time you proposed until the meeting organizer accepts or rejects your proposed time.

Other Response Options

The **Respond** command, found in the **Respond** command group, provides a number of other response options that do not pertain to the meeting invite. When you choose one of these response options, the meeting request is not accepted or declined. You can choose to respond to the sender in a different manner before reacting to the meeting request. The other response options include:

- **Reply**
- **Reply All**
- **Forward**
- **Reply with IM**
- **Reply All with IM**
- **Call**
- **Forward as Attachment**

	Note: Outlook on the Web When responding to meeting invitations, you have three response options: **Accept, Tentative,** and **Decline**. Unlike in the desktop application, you do not have the opportunity to add comments to your responses or propose a new time.

	Note: You know how to update information for a meeting, but what if that update or reschedule only applies to one instance in a recurring meeting? For more information, check out the LearnTO **Reschedule One Occurrence in a Recurring Meeting Series** presentation from the **LearnTO** tile on the CHOICE Course screen.

	Access the Checklist tile on your CHOICE Course screen for reference information and job aids on How to Manage Meetings.

ACTIVITY 5-3
Responding to a Meeting Request

Scenario

Now that Develetech has implemented Outlook as its email client, more people are beginning to schedule meetings through the calendar. There are a number of meeting invites in your Inbox that you need to respond to.

There are two Vacation Policy Discussions that have been scheduled, and you can choose which one to attend. You would rather attend the forum on Thursday morning. You need to decline the invitation for the Wednesday meeting and accept the invitation for the Thursday meeting.

---

1. Decline the Vacation Policy Discussion Forum 1 meeting invitation.
    a) On the **Navigation** bar, select **Mail** to open your Inbox.
    b) In the message list, find and select the meeting request from Shanelle Newsom with the subject "Vacation Policy Discussion Forum 1."
    c) In the invitation in the **Reading** pane, select **Decline** and choose **Send the Response Now**.

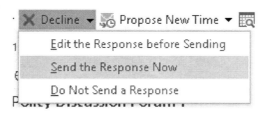

    d) Verify that the meeting invitation item has been removed from your message list.

2. Accept the Vacation Policy Discussion Forum 2 meeting invitation.
    a) In the message list, find and select the meeting request from Shanelle Newsom with the subject "Vacation Policy Discussion Forum 2."
    b) In the invitation in the **Reading** pane, select **Accept** and choose **Edit the Response before Sending**.

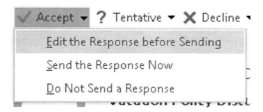

    c) In the **Accepted: Vacation Policy Discussion Forum 2 - Meeting Response** form that opens, type *I'll see you there!* in the message body, and select **Send**.
    d) Verify that the meeting invitation item has been removed from your message list.
    e) On the **Navigation** bar, select **Calendar**.
    f) In the calendar grid, select the **Forward** arrow ▸ to advance to the following week.
    g) Verify that the Vacation Policy Discussion Forum 2 meeting appears on your calendar on the following Thursday at 10:00 a.m.

ACTIVITY 5-4
Proposing a New Time for a Meeting

Scenario
You have been invited to a meeting on the following day by Angie Blumquist for 8 a.m. You can't attend a meeting at that time, so you want to propose a new time for the meeting to occur.

Decline the Meet to Discuss Candidates meeting and propose a new time of 8:30 a.m.

a) On the **Navigation** bar, select **Mail**.

b) In the message list, find and select the meeting request from Angie Blumquist with the subject "Meet to Discuss Candidates."

c) In the invitation in the **Reading** pane, select **Propose New Time** and choose **Decline and Propose New Time**.

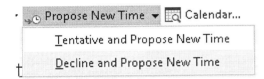

d) In the **Propose New Time: Meet to Discuss Candidates** dialog box, in the **Meeting start time** field, select **9:00 AM** from the drop-down.

e) Verify that the **Meeting end time** field has automatically updated to **10:00 a.m.**

f) Verify in the **Propose New Time** dialog box that Angie is free and available to meet during the time you selected.

g) Select **Propose Time**.

h) In the **New Time Proposed: Meet to Discuss Candidates - Meeting Response** message that automatically opens, in the message body, type *Angie, can we meet at 9 a.m. instead? I have to drop Jason off at daycare that morning.*

i) Select **Send**.

j) Verify that the meeting invitation item has been removed from your message list.

ACTIVITY 5-5
Creating a Recurring Meeting Request

Scenario

As a lead on the recruitment team for Develetech's latest recruitment effort, you have been tasked with scheduling a weekly meeting for the entire team. You decide to schedule a recurring meeting on Fridays of each week, beginning with this week.

1. Open and create a new meeting with the recruitment team to discuss the recruitment effort.

   a) In the **Navigation** bar, select **Calendar**.

   b) In the **New** command group, select **New Meeting**.

   New
   Meeting

   c) In the subject line, type *Weekly Recruitment Team Meeting*

   d) Select **To**. The **Select Attendees and Resources: Global Address List** dialog box will open.

   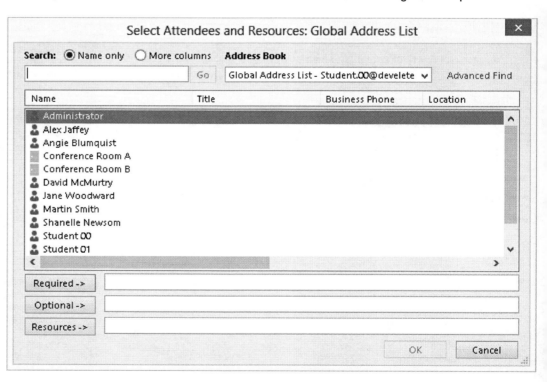

   e) Find and select **Alex Jaffey** and select **Required**.

   f) Add Jane Woodward and Shanelle Newsom as required attendees.

   g) Add Angie Blumquist as an optional attendee.

   h) Select **OK** and verify that the **To** field in the meeting form has been updated with all the attendees.

i)   In the **Location** field, select the **Rooms** button.

j)   Select **Conference Room B** in the list, select **Rooms**, and select **OK**.

k)   On the **MEETING** tab, in the **Show** command group, select **Scheduling Assistant**.

Scheduling
Assistant

l)   In the **Start time** field, select the calendar icon ⊞ and select this coming Friday. Verify that the date in the **End time** field changes to the same date.

m)   In the **Start time** field, select **2:00 PM** from the drop-down.

n)   In the **End time** field, select **4:00 PM (2 hours)** from the drop-down.

o)   Verify that all of the required attendees appear to be free and available during the scheduled meeting time, and that there are no conflicts.

2.   Make the meeting a recurring meeting for the next five weeks.

a)   In the **Options** command group, select **Recurrence**. ↻ Recurrence

b)   In the **Range of recurrence** section, select the **End after** radio button and change the number of occurrences to **5**.

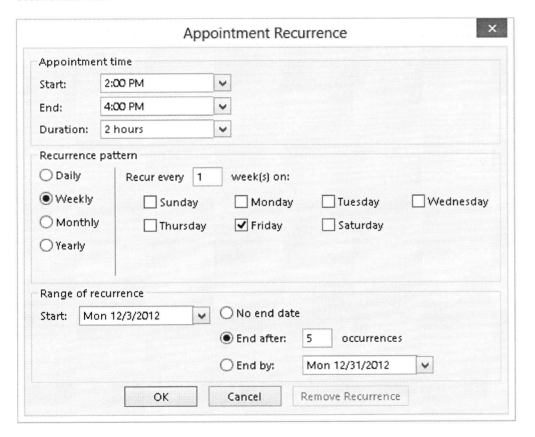

c)   Select **OK**.

d)   Select **Send**. ⌨ Send

TOPIC D

Print Your Calendar

Now that you have scheduled both appointments and meetings in your calendar, your calendar should be a good representation of when you are free and when you are busy. There might be times when you want to print your calendar or calendar entries to have a hard copy of the information, rather than having to access Outlook to see it. In this topic, you will print your calendar.

Once you get used to using the **Calendar** workspace to keep track of your appointments and meetings, you will have a much better handle on managing your time efficiently. With your calendar up-to-date, you can use the **Print** option to print hard copies of your calendar or calender entries so you have them to look at when you are not able to view them in Outlook.

Calendar Print Styles

When printing your calendar, there are a number of styles from which you can choose, ranging from printing the details for a single event, to printing the details for all events in a single month. When you select **FILE→Print** from the **Calendar** workspace, the print styles are displayed in the **Settings** section in the **Backstage View**.

Print Style	Description
Memo Style	Available only when a calendar event is selected or opened. It prints the details of the specific event.
Daily Style	Prints the events for a single day, broken down by hourly time slots. Also includes the **Daily Task List** and any available **Notes** for the day.
Weekly Agenda Styles	Prints the events for the entire week (Monday through Sunday), in the form of a daily agenda. Each day of the week has its own slot, with that day's events listed with their times, locations, and other details.
Weekly Calendar Style	Prints the events for the entire week (Monday through Sunday), in the form of calendar entries with hourly time slots. Each day of the week has its own set of time slots, with the events of the day listed in the appropriate time slot with location, attendees, and other details.
Monthly Style	Prints the events for the entire month. Events are listed in their appropriate day of the month, with important details for the events like times and locations.
Tri-fold Style	Prints a three-paneled view of events for both a single day and week. The first panel is the events for a single day in the **Daily Style**. The second panel is the **Daily Task** list for that day. The third panel is the weekly agenda for the week in which the selected day falls in the **Weekly Agenda Style**.
Calendar Details Style	Prints the details for all events scheduled in the calendar in a daily agenda style. Whenever there is an event on the calendar, that day and the events that occur on that day—with their important details included—are printed.

Note: Outlook on the Web

When you print your Outlook calendar from the online app, you can choose the type of view, the layout, and the begin and end times that you want to print. You also have the option to print a detailed agenda with the calendar.

Access the Checklist tile on your CHOICE Course screen for reference information and job aids on How to Print Your Calendar.

ACTIVITY 5-6
Printing Your Calendar

Scenario

To help everyone at Develetech keep better track of their colleagues' availabilities and to know where people are to get in touch with them, senior management has asked that each employee print and display their calendar outside their office. You need to print your calendar for the work week.

Print your calendar for the current work week.

a) On the ribbon, select **FILE→Print**.

b) In the **Settings** section, select **Weekly Agenda Style**.

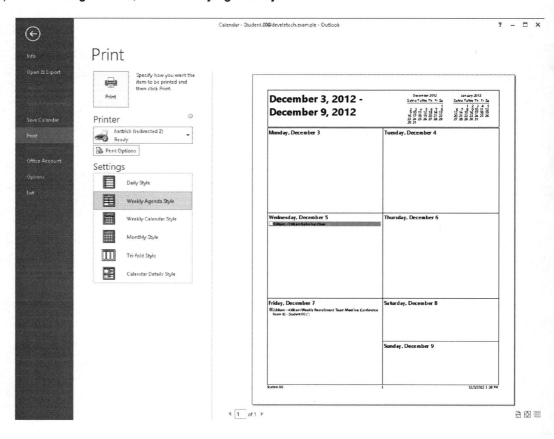

c) View what your calendar will look like in this style in the preview pane to the right.

d) Select **Print**.

Summary

In this lesson, you used the **Calendar** workspace in Outlook to manage your appointments and meetings. Using the features available in the **Calendar** workspace helps you keep track of your own personal calendar events, and both personal appointments and meetings you have scheduled during work hours with your coworkers. Keeping your calendar up-to-date also allows your coworkers who meet with you to know when you are available and when you are not. Managing your calendar can help you manage your time more effectively and efficiently.

How do you think you will be using the Outlook Calendar workspace most frequently: will you be on the receiving end of meeting requests, or will you be the one sending and managing meeting requests? How do you think using Outlook will differ for those two different uses of the application?

How do you anticipate you will use the features of the Calendar workspace, such as appointments versus meetings, and recurrences, reminders, printing your calendar, and more, to best manage your time?

 Note: Check your CHOICE Course screen for opportunities to interact with your classmates, peers, and the larger CHOICE online community about the topics covered in this course or other topics you are interested in. From the Course screen you can also access available resources for a more continuous learning experience.

6 Managing Your Contacts

Lesson Time: 40 minutes

Lesson Objectives

In this lesson, you will:

- Create and update contacts.

- View and organize contacts.

Lesson Introduction

You have used the **Mail** workspace to manage your email communications and have used the **Calendar** workspace to manage your appointments and meetings. Those Microsoft® Office Outlook® items have been sent between you and other recipients, and Outlook also provides a way for you to manage those people you interact with often. In this lesson, you will manage your contacts.

If there are people with whom you communicate often, or with whom you meet frequently, you likely have saved their contact information somewhere for easy access. Just like Outlook provides you with an workspace in which to send emails and meeting invitations to those people, it also provides you with a way to create and store their contact information in a easily accessible location. The **Contacts** workspace can help you manage those people with whom you interact on a regular basis.

TOPIC A

Create and Update Contacts

Now that you are familiar with the email and calendar functions in Outlook, you will likely find yourself using the application more to interact with your recipients. Saving contact information for the people you communicate with the most will help you to perform those functions more quickly and easily. In this topic, you will create and update contacts.

As you begin to use Outlook more to communicate and schedule meetings, you may find that the number of people you interact with has increased exponentially. How do you keep track of all the people you have interacted with? And how do you manage all of their contact information to make those interactions as easy as possible? With the **Contacts** workspace in Outlook, you can create and update a list of your contacts quickly and easily.

Contacts

A *contact* is any person with whom you need to communicate for business or personal reasons. Contact information for a person in your contacts may include his or her name, physical addresses, phone numbers, email addresses, and other information that can help you communicate with that person, such as websites or instant message addresses.

The People Hub

The *People Hub* is the new default view for your contacts in Outlook 2013. In the People Hub, all of the contacts you have saved or added appear, even contacts you have added from your social networks. Your contacts now display using an updated **People Card,** which aggregates information about that contact from multiple sources into a single location.

Your list of contacts is displayed in the **Content** pane. By default, the **Reading** pane is turned on, and the contact information for the selected contact displays in the **Reading** pane. There are three tabs available on the **Reading** pane:

- The **CONTACT** tab displays the contact information you have added and saved for that contact. From this tab, you can also interact with your contacts by scheduling a meeting with them, sending them an email, or viewing their Outlook Profile.
- The **NOTES** tab displays any notes you have saved in the Contact form or People Hub location about the contact.
- The **WHAT'S NEW** tab displays any new information about the contact that the contact has added to their online social networks.

You can also select **Edit** in the **Reading** pane to open the contact information for the selected contact and edit their information directly in the **Reading** pane.

 Note: When you select **Outlook Profile** on the **CONTACT** tab, the **Contact** form for the contact is opened. You can edit the contact information for your contact in the **Contact** form, or you can edit it using the **Edit** option in the **Reading** pane. Both locations will be updated with the modified information.

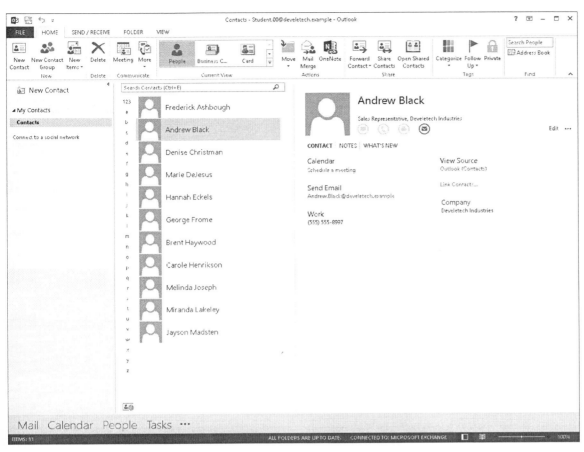

Figure 6-1: The People Hub displays information for all of your contacts, including those you have added from your social networks.

Note: Outlook on the Web

Using the online app, you can create, view, and edit contacts using procedures that are similar to the ones used in the desktop application. To view your contacts, select the **App Launcher** icon and then select the **People** tile. The **People** page is a scaled-down version of the desktop People Hub. Your contact folders appear in the left pane, list of contacts in the middle, and the contact details in the right pane. You can use the **Filter** menu at the top of the middle pane to change how the list is sorted and displayed.

The Contact Form

Your contacts are created and managed using the **Contact** form. When you select **New Contact** from the **New** command group, a blank **Contact** form opens.

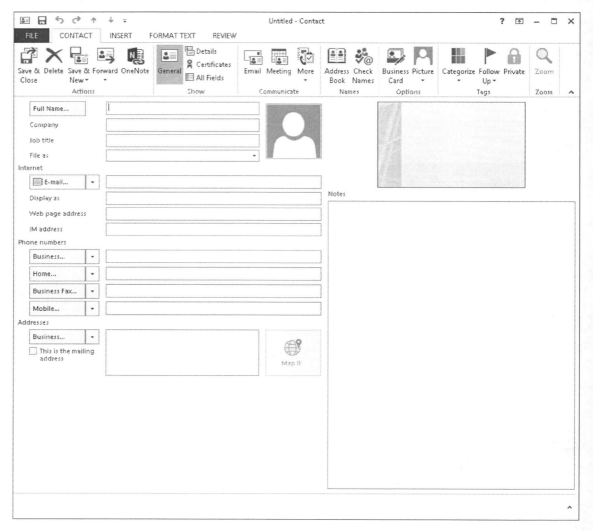

Figure 6-2: Contact information is entered into a Contact form.

The **Contact** form has a number of fields where you enter the contact information and details for the person you are creating a contact record for.

- In the **Full Name** field, you can enter the first and last name of the contact.
- In the **Company** field, you can enter the name of the company or organization where the contact works.
- In the **Job title** field, you can enter the job title that the contact holds.
- In the **File as** field, you can choose the way in which the contact will be filed in your contacts list. The default **File as** method is last name, first name.
- In the **Email** field, you can enter the primary email address you will use to communicate with the contact. You can add additional emails by selecting the drop-down and entering in another email address for **Email 2** or **Email 3**.
- In the **Display as** field, you can choose how the contact is displayed when you email them. The default **Display as** method is full name (email address).
- In the **Web page address** field, you can enter the URL of the contact's website, if they have one.
- In the **IM address** field, you can enter the Instant Messenger name of the contact, if they have one.
- In the **Phone Numbers** section, you can enter the contact's business, home, business fax, and mobile phone numbers in their respective fields.

- In the **Addresses** section, you can enter the contact's business address. You can add additional addresses, such as their residence, by selecting the drop-down and entering in another address for **Home** or **Other**.
- In the **Notes** field, you can enter any additional information pertaining to the contact that might be useful to you.

The Details Command on the Contact Form

If you need or want to add additional details about your contact, on the **Contact** tab, in the **Show** command group, select **Details**.

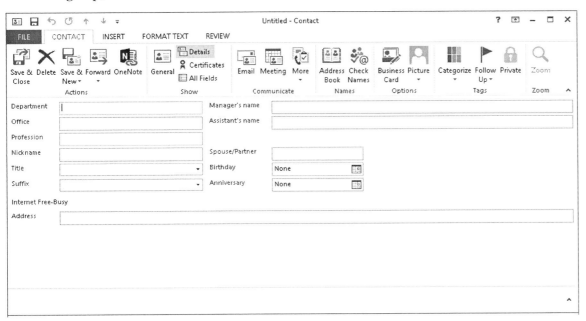

Figure 6–3: The Details section allows you to add additional information about a contact.

The **Details** section of the **Contact** form allows you to add additional information about the contact, including their:

- **Department**
- **Office**
- **Profession**
- **Manager's name**
- **Assistant's name**
- **Nickname**
- **Title**
- **Suffix**
- **Spouse or partner's name**
- **Birthday**
- **Anniversary**
- **Internet Free-Busy address**

Note: Outlook on the Web

When creating a new contact, it is important to select the contact folder first and then create the contact. Moving contacts to another folder is not possible. You can, however, delete the contact and then re-create it in the desired folder.

Access the Checklist tile on your CHOICE Course screen for reference information and job aids on How to Create and Update Contacts.

Secondary Address Books

By default, the contacts you create are stored in the default address book that is created during an installation of Outlook. However, you can create secondary address books in Outlook. *Secondary address books* are additional address books that you can create, name at your discretion, and use to store your contacts. You can create as many secondary address books as you would like to help you organize your contact list.

Import Contacts

You can import contacts from other locations, including your other email clients, into Outlook and store them in your secondary address books. To import contacts into your secondary address book, you must save them as a suitable file type to import, and format the file to match the fields in Outlook. Common file types to use to import contacts include Microsoft® Excel® (.xls) files or Comma Separated Value (.csv) files.

Note: Outlook on the Web

This feature is not available in the online app. If you want to import contacts, you must use Outlook 2013.

Access the Checklist tile on your CHOICE Course screen for reference information and job aids on How to Manage Secondary Address Books and Import Contacts.

ACTIVITY 6-1
Creating and Updating Contacts

Scenario

Develetech is using a global address list in Outlook, so there is always a contacts list of all employees available to you that make communicating with your coworkers very easy. But you also want to manage your own contacts list, where you can keep a robust list of contacts for people you communicate with professionally, including both internal and external contacts. You have a number of contacts that you want to add, update, or remove from your list.

- Josh Kincaid is a customer of yours, and you communicate with him often. You want to add Josh as a contact so you can easily communicate with him.
- Sylvia Alvarez-Ortiz is a coworker at Develetech, and while you communicate with her frequently, you haven't added her to your contacts list yet. She recently sent you an email via Outlook, and you want to add her to your contacts list from her email.
- Earlier in the week, one of your coworkers, David, sent an email that included new contact information for your new representative at your corporate travel provider. Rather than creating a new contact, you want to save the attached contact to your contacts list.
- Melinda Joseph, your friend and a coworker at Develetech, has recently moved. You want to update her contact information in your contacts list to include her new home phone number.
- George Frome recently retired from Develetech, but you still have him in your contacts list. You want to delete the contact for George.

---

1. On the **Navigation** bar, select **People**.

2. Add Josh Kincaid as a new contact.
   a) On the **HOME** tab, in the **New** command group, select **New Contact**.

New
Contact

   b) A new contact form will open, with the title "Untitled - Contact."
   c) In the **Full Name** field, type *Josh Kincaid*
   d) In the **Company** field, type *Bit by Bit Fitness*
   e) Verify that the **File as** field automatically populated and displays **Kincaid, Josh**.
   f) In the **Internet** section, in the **E-mail** field, type *jkincaid@bxbfitness.example*
   g) Select in the **Display as** field, and verify that it automatically populates with **Josh Kincaid (jkincaid@bxbfitness.example)**.
   h) In the **Phone numbers** section, in the **Business** field, type *(555) 555-7070*

Note: If location information has not been established in Windows, the **Location Information** dialog box may display when you try to add a phone number. If so, leave the **What country/region are you in now?** field at the default of **United States**, and in the **What area code (or city code) are you in now?** type *555* and select **OK**. Then, in the **Phone and Modem Options** dialog box, select **OK**.

      i)   Select in the **Notes** section and verify that the business card has automatically populated with all the contact information for Josh.

      j)   Select **Save & Close**.

Save &
Close

      k)   Verify that Josh Kincaid now appears in your list of contacts in the People Hub.

3.   Create a contact for Sylvia Alvarez-Ortiz from her email message.

      a)   On the **Navigation** bar, select **Mail**.

      b)   In the message list, find and select the email message from Sylvia with the subject line "New Product Rollout."

      c)   In the message content in the **Reading** pane, hover over Sylvia's name in the message header until the pop-out for the contact appears.

      d)   On the pop-out, select the **Open Contact Card** down-arrow.

      e)   In the **People Card,** select the **Add to Outlook Contacts** button.

      f)   A People Card for Sylvia Alvarez-Ortis will open, with her name and email address populated.

      g)   Select the add another field icon ⊕ next to the **Phone** field and from the drop-down, select **Work**.

      h)   In the new **Work** field that was added, type *(555) 555-8991*.

      i)   Select **Save**.

      j)   Close the People Card for Sylvia.

4.   Save Robert Chisolm's contact information from the email message into your contact list.

      a)   In the message list, find and select the email message from David McMurtry with the subject line "New Travel Company and Contact."

      b)   In the message content in the **Reading** pane, select the attached contact card titled "Robert Chisolm." A preview of Robert's contact form appears in the **Reading** pane.

      c)   Select the attached contact card, and drag it to **People** on the **Navigation** bar.

      d)   The cursor will display a plus sign, indicating that you can drop the file into **People**.

      e)   On the **Navigation** bar, drop the card into **People**.

      f)   Verify that Robert Chisolm's business card now appears in your list of contacts.

5.   Update Melinda Joseph's contact information to include her new phone number.

      a)   In your list of contacts, find and select Melinda Joseph.

      b)   In the **Reading** pane, select **Edit**.

      c)   Select the add another field icon ⊕ next to the **Phone** field and from the drop-down, select **Home**.

      d)   In the **Home** field, type *(555) 555-6280*

      e)   Select **Save**.

6.   Delete George Frome from your contact list.

      a)   In your list of contacts, find and select George Frome.

      b)   On the **HOME** tab, in the **Delete** command group, select **Delete**.

Delete

      c)   Verify that George Frome no longer appears in your list of contacts.

TOPIC B

View and Organize Contacts

Once you have added contacts to your **People** workspace, you will need to be able to view and organize those contacts in an easy and streamlined manner. Knowing how to change the layout of the **People** workspace and other ways you can organize your contacts will enable you to locate and work with the contact information for people you communicate with often. In this topic, you will view and organize your contacts.

In addition to the contacts you may have access to as part of a **Global Address List** for your company, the **People** workspace and the address books you can create for yourself are additional places for you to store and organize the contact information for those people you communicate with frequently. Knowing how to view this information and organize it in an easily accessible manner make it easier for you to manage your contacts.

Electronic Business Cards

An electronic business card is a feature in Outlook that can be used to easily create, view, and share contact information with others. An electronic business card looks just like a printed business card, and displays any contact information that has been saved for the specific contact. Just like a printed business card, the design of the electronic business card can be customized to include a background, images, or a company logo.

You can create your own personal electronic business card (or multiple business cards) and share them with your contacts by attaching them to your emails. You can also include your electronic business card in your email signature, making it easier for people you communicate with to view and save your contact information.

> **Note: Outlook on the Web**
>
> This feature is not available in the online app. You must use the desktop application to create business cards.

Contact Views

Outlook provides a variety of ways in which you can display the contacts in your contact list. These view options are found on the **HOME** tab, in the **Current View** command group.

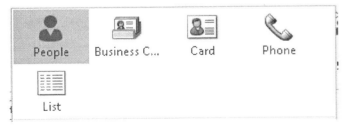

Figure 6-4: Contact views provide different ways to display your contacts.

- **People** displays your contacts in the People Hub. Your contacts are listed in ascending alphabetical order (A to Z) by last name, and the contact information for a selected contact is displayed in the **Reading** pane.
- **Business Card** displays each of your contacts as a business card with their contact information, in ascending alphabetical order (A to Z) by last name.

- **Card** displays a small card for each of your contacts, in descending alphabetical order (Z to A) by last name, with the contact information for the contact selected displayed in a **Reading** pane below the contact list.
- **Phone** displays a list of your contacts with business phone numbers as the primary category, in ascending alphabetical order by last name.
- **List** displays a list of your contacts, grouped together by a common category such as a company, each group in ascending alphabetical order by last name.

The default view for the contacts in your contact list is the **People** view, which displays your contacts using the People Hub.

Sort Options

By default, your contacts are sorted in alphabetical order. Depending on the **Contact** view, this may be in either ascending or descending order. You can modify the sort options in a number of ways:

- The **Reverse sort** command, found on the **VIEW** tab in the **Arrangement** command group, will reverse the order in which your contacts are sorted. If by default your contacts are sorted in ascending alphabetical order, using the **Reverse sort** option will list them in descending alphabetical order. This is helpful if you need to quickly find a contact at the opposite end of the sort order.

- You can also configure advanced sort settings for the different contact views using the **Sort** options in the **Advanced View Settings** options. To access the **Sort** options, select the **VIEW** tab, and in the **Current View** command group, select **View Settings**. In the **Advanced View Settings** dialog box, select **Sort**. In the **Sort** settings, you can configure up to four ways in which to sort your items, and in what manner (ascending versus descending).

Note: Outlook on the Web

You can use the **Filter** menu to change how your contact list is sorted and displayed.

The Find Tool

The **Find** tool in Outlook allows you to search for and find contacts in any of your address books based on a keyword search. When you type a keyword, such as the first name of a contact, into the **Search People** text box, found in the **Find** command group on the **HOME** tab, Outlook will search your contacts for that keyword, display a list of the contacts available that include the keyword term, and allow you to select and display the **Contact** form for a particular contact.

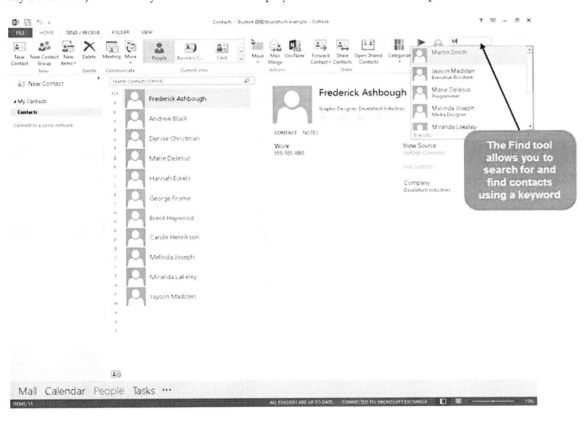

Figure 6-5: The Find tool.

Search Terms

When you enter a keyword, partial keyword, or phrase in the **Search People** text box, Outlook looks in the **Contacts** folder for a word or phrase that matches the word entered. Outlook will only search for partial names, first or last names, email addresses, display as names, and company names.

 Note: Outlook on the Web

In the online app, the **Search** box appears at the top of the left pane. You can search by text or numbers and further refine the search by selecting a specific folder or directory to search.

 Access the Checklist tile on your **CHOICE** Course screen for reference information and job aids on **How to View and Organize Contacts.**

ACTIVITY 6-2
Viewing and Organizing Your Contacts

Scenario

As you create and save more contacts into your contact lists, you find that it is becoming more difficult to keep track of all of the people you communicate with. You want to use the different views available in Outlook to display and view your contacts, and utilize the options available to you to help organize your contacts.

1. Explore the different views available for displaying your contacts.
   a) On the **HOME** tab on the ribbon, in the **Current View** command group, if necessary, select the **More** drop-down ⬇ to display all the views available for your contacts.
   b) Verify that **People** is selected by default, and that your contacts are being displayed in the People Hub.
   c) In the **Current View** command group, select **Business Card,** and examine how your contacts appear listed as electronic business cards.
   d) Select **Card** and examine how your contacts look using the **Card** view.
   e) Select **Phone** and examine how your contacts look using the **Phone** view.
   f) Select **List** and examine how your contacts look using the **List** view.

2. Select **Business Card** as your contact view.

3. Change the way in which your contacts are sorted in the contact list.
   a) Verify that, by default, your contacts are sorted alphabetically by last name and listed in ascending order, from A to Z.
   b) Select the **VIEW** tab.
   c) In the **Arrangement** command group, select **Reverse Sort**. ↑↓ Reverse Sort
   d) Verify that your contacts are now sorted alphabetically by last name, but listed in descending order.

4. Display the **Reading** pane to view details for your contacts without having to open the contact.
   a) On the **VIEW** tab, in the **Layout** command group, select **Reading** pane and select **Right**.

   b) Select any business card in the contacts list and view the contact's detailed information that appears in the **Reading** pane.

5. Select the **HOME** tab and select the **People** view to return to the default view of the People Hub.

Contacts Print Styles

When printing your contacts, there are a number of styles from which you can choose, ranging from printing the details for a single contacts to printing an entire address book worth of contacts. When you select **FILE→Print** from the **People** workspace, the print styles are displayed in the **Settings** section in the **Backstage View**.

Print Style	Description
Card Style	Prints an address book of all your contacts, with each contact displaying as a business card with available contact information. Contacts are listed in alphabetical order, but depending on the view selected, they may be listed in either ascending or descending order.
Small Booklet Style	Prints a small-sized booklet of your address book, with each contact and their contact information. Contacts are listed and grouped alphabetically by last name, but depending on the view selected, they may be listed in either ascending or descending order.
Medium Booklet Style	Prints a medium-sized booklet of your address book, with each contact and their contact information. Contacts are listed and grouped alphabetically by last name, but depending on the view selected, they may be listed in either ascending or descending order.
Memo Style	Prints the contact information for a single contact. By default, the first contact in an address book is selected and its information is displayed. To print a specific contact's information, you must first select the contact in the list before accessing the **Print** option.
Phone Directory Style	Prints your contacts like a phone book, with only a name and any available telephone numbers for the contact. Contacts are listed and grouped alphabetically by last name, but depending on the view selected, they may be listed in either ascending or descending order.
Table Style	Is the only available print style when viewing your contact list with either the **Phone** or **List** view. Prints all of your contacts as a table that includes their contact information. The print style matches the view selected.

Note: Outlook on the Web

This feature is not available in the online app. If you want to print your contact list, you must use the desktop application. You can use the web browser's **Print** command, but you only have control over the page settings and not the content being displayed on the page.

Access the Checklist tile on your **CHOICE Course** screen for reference information and job aids on **How to Print Contacts**.

ACTIVITY 6–3
Printing Your Contacts

Scenario

You have created robust contact lists in Outlook for both your personal and professional contacts. You want to print hard copies of your contacts that you can have on hand in your office and at home in case you need to contact someone and you cannot access your contacts in Outlook.

Explore the print options available and select one for printing all of the contacts in the **Contacts** folder.

a) If necessary, on the **Navigation** bar, select **People**.

b) On the ribbon, select **FILE→Print**.

c) In the **Settings** section, verify that **Card Style** is selected automatically, and examine how the contacts would be printed in the preview pane at the right.

 Note: You can zoom in on the print preview if you need to. Your cursor will appear as a magnifying glass when you hover over the preview; select an area of the screen with it to zoom in on that area.

d) In the **Settings** section, select **Small Booklet Style,** and examine how the contacts would be printed in the preview pane at the right.

e) Select the other available styles and examine how the contacts would be printed in the preview pane.

f) Select the print style of your liking, and select **Print**.

g) If you receive a **Microsoft Outlook** dialog box informing you about double-sided printing, select **Yes**.

Summary

In this lesson, you used the **People** workspace in Outlook to manage your contacts. Using the features available in your **People** workspace, you can create, maintain and organize the contact information for those people that you communicate or interact with most often. When your contacts are up-to-date, well-maintained and well-organized, using the other Outlook features like sending emails or meeting requests becomes even easier.

Do you think you will maintain your own address book of contacts? Will you use contacts more for personal or professional contacts?

When might you print your contacts? Why might the print feature be useful to you?

 Note: Check your CHOICE Course screen for opportunities to interact with your classmates, peers, and the larger CHOICE online community about the topics covered in this course or other topics you are interested in. From the Course screen you can also access available resources for a more continuous learning experience.

7 Working With Tasks and Notes

Lesson Time: 30 minutes

Lesson Objectives

In this lesson, you will:

- Manage tasks.

- Manage notes.

Lesson Introduction

You have used the other workspaces in Microsoft® Office Outlook®—**Mail, Calendar,** and **People**—to manage your communications with other people. Outlook also provides you with two other features, **Tasks** and **Notes,** that you can use to help manage your own personal assignments and communications with yourself. In this lesson, you will work with tasks and notes.

The emails and meeting requests that you send, receive, and manage among yourself and your recipients is fairly easy to navigate in Outlook. But how do you keep track of assignments or information that you need to remember, but that don't necessarily involve other people? Maybe they are only specific to you? Outlook also provides two features to help you manage and organize these very personal activities: **Tasks** and **Notes**.

TOPIC A

Manage Tasks

Now that you are using Outlook to send emails, schedule meetings, and keep track of all your contacts, you might find yourself with more tasks that you have to complete. Outlook provides a handy way for you to schedule, manage, and view personal tasks that need to be completed. In this topic, you will manage your tasks in Outlook using tasks.

As you become more familiar with all the features and functionalities of Outlook, it is likely that you will have more emails to respond to or more meetings to attend. It might be easier for people to assign you tasks and activities for you to complete, and you may find yourself with more tasks to complete than ever! In anticipation of your needs to keep track of all of these tasks, Outlook includes the Tasks feature. With Tasks, you can schedule and track personal tasks for yourself, to make sure they are completed in a timely manner.

Tasks

A *task* in Outlook is an action item, activity, or piece of work that is assigned to you and that must be completed within a certain time frame. You can assign a task to yourself or to other people, and other people can assign a task to you. The **Tasks** workspace in Outlook is where you can create and manage the tasks that you assign to yourself or are assigned to you using the **Tasks** feature.

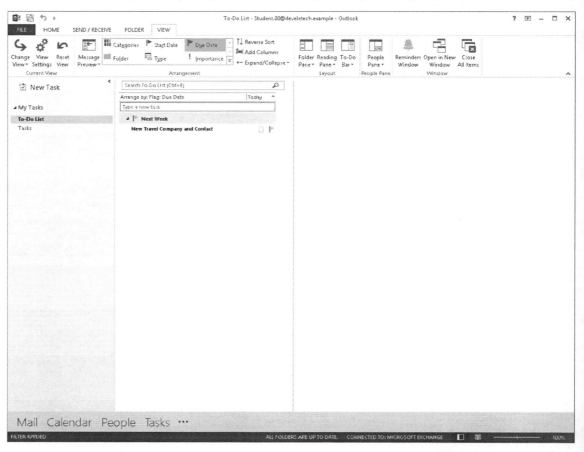

Figure 7–1: The Tasks workspace in Outlook is where you can create and manage the tasks you need to complete.

Note: Outlook on the Web

Using the online app, you can create, view, and edit tasks; however, if you need to assign or share tasks with others, you must use the desktop application. To view your tasks, select the **App Launcher** icon and then select the **Tasks** tile. The **Tasks** page is a simplified version of the desktop Tasks view.

Note: In this course, *Microsoft® Office Outlook® 2013: Part 1 (Desktop/Office 365™)*, we only cover tasks that you have assigned to yourself for organizational purposes. For more information about managing activities by assigning tasks to others or replying to tasks that have been assigned to you, please see the *Microsoft® Office Outlook® 2013: Part 2* course.

Task Form

Tasks are created and managed using the **Task** form. When you select **New Task** from the **New** command group, a blank **Task** form opens.

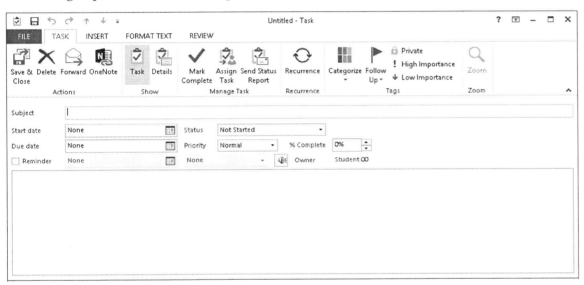

Figure 7-2: Information about a task you are assigning to yourself is entered into a Task form.

The **Task** form has a number of fields where you enter the necessary information about the task assignment.

- In the **Subject** field, you enter a brief description of the task.
- In the **Start date** field, you select the date when the task is scheduled to begin from the calendar.
- In the **Due date** field, you select the date by which the task must be completed from the calendar.
- From the **Status** drop-down, you select the current status of the assignment: **Not Started, In Progress, Completed, Waiting on someone else,** or **Deferred**.
- From the **Priority** drop-down, you select the priority level of the assignment: **Low, Normal,** or **High**.
- In the **% Complete** field, you use the spin boxes to select a percentage of completion for the assignment.
- If a reminder for the task is needed, you can check the **Reminder** check box and select a date and time from the drop-downs for the reminder notification.
- The **Owner** field displays the owner of the task (if you assigned the task to yourself, it is your name; if the task was assigned to you by someone else, it will be the name of the person who assigned it.)
- In the message body, you can enter any specific information about the assignment.

Task Views

The tasks that are assigned to you, whether by yourself or by others, can be viewed in three locations in the Outlook interface: in the **Content** pane within the **Tasks** workspace (whether in the **To-Do List** folder or the **Tasks** folder), in the **Tasks** component on the **To-Do Bar** in any of the Outlook workspaces, and in the **Tasks** pane in the calendar if the **Daily Task List** has been made visible.

Within the **Tasks** workspace, you can view the details of the tasks assigned to you in a variety of ways. These views are found on the **HOME** tab on the ribbon, in the **Current View** command group.

Figure 7-3: The tasks views available in the Current View command group.

Views include:

- **Detailed** displays your tasks and any of the details the task has been given, and includes the subject, status, due date, any dates it was modified, the date it was completed, the location in a folder, any color categories assigned to the task, if the task was flagged for follow-up, and information that belongs in any other columns you may have added to your sort bar when customizing your environment.
- **Simple List** displays your tasks as a simple list and includes the subject of the task, the due date, and any color categories or flags that have been assigned to the task.
- **To-Do List** displays your tasks in the same manner that they appear in the **To-Do Bar**, and can be arranged according to their type, importance, start date, due date, or categories.
- **Prioritized** displays your tasks according to the priority that has been assigned to them. Tasks are grouped by high, normal, and low priorities.
- **Active** displays any of your tasks that are still active and ongoing tasks, and includes the subject, status, due date, percent complete, and any color categories or flags that have been assigned to the task.
- **Completed** displays only the tasks assigned to you that have been completed, and includes the subject, due date, date completed, and any color categories or flags that were assigned to the task.
- **Today** displays any tasks that are assigned for the current date, and includes the subject, due date, and any color categories or flags that have been assigned to the task.
- **Next 7 Days** displays any tasks that have been scheduled for the next seven days, and includes the subject, status, due date, percent complete, and any color categories or flags that have been assigned to the task.
- **Overdue** displays any tasks assigned to you that are overdue/past their due date, and includes the subject, status, due date, percent complete, and any color categories or flags that have been assigned to the task.
- **Assigned** displays any tasks that have been assigned to you by someone else, and includes the subject, owner, due date, status, and any flags that have been assigned to the task.

Server Tasks

Microsoft® Outlook®, Project®, and SharePoint® can all be used together to help synchronize tasks that are assigned to members of a project team. These tasks that are synchronized using these tools can be displayed using the **Server Tasks** view. The **Server Tasks** view includes the subject, assigned persons, status, priority level, due date, and folder location for the task.

Note: Outlook on the Web

You can sort your tasks by selecting the **Items by** menu that contains a variety of sort criteria.

Task Options

When creating and assigning a task, there are a number of options you can enable for the assignment. These options include:

- **Recurrence:** Tasks, like appointments and meetings, can be scheduled as recurring. If the assignment happens on a regular basis, such as daily or weekly, you can select the **Recurrence** option and configure the task to be a recurring task.
- **Regeneration:** You can set the next task in a recurrence to only occur if the previous task was marked as completed.
- **Categorize:** You can assign a color category to your tasks to help you organize and visually keep track of your tasks.
- **Follow Up:** You can flag tasks for follow-up to help keep track of which items need to be followed up with an action or completed by a certain time.
- **Private:** You can mark a task as private so that other people who may have access to your calendar cannot see the details of your task.
- **Priority:** levels: You can mark a task as **High Importance** or **Low Importance** to help convey to yourself or others the priority level of the task.

Access the Checklist tile on your CHOICE Course screen for reference information and job aids on How to Manage Tasks.

ACTIVITY 7–1
Managing Tasks

Scenario

As a key member of the recruitment team hiring new multimedia designers for Develetech, you have been assigned with many specific tasks regarding the recruitment effort. You have already scheduled weekly team meetings with the recruitment team, and you think it is a good idea to have an agenda with the items to discuss at each meeting. In fact, you want to develop the agenda the day before the weekly meeting and send it out to the team to review prior to the meeting. You can use the **Tasks** option in Outlook to manage this as a personal task for yourself.

---

1. Create a Prepare Weekly Meeting Agenda recurring task.

   a) On the **Navigation** bar, select **Tasks**.

   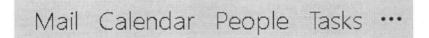

   b) On the **HOME** tab, select **New Task**.

   New
   Task

   c) In the **Subject** field, type *Prepare Weekly Meeting Agenda*

   d) In the **Start date** field, select the calendar icon ▦ and in the calendar, select the following Thursday.

   e) Verify that the **Due date** field is updated to the date you just selected. Leave the **Due date** as is.

   f) Select the **Priority** drop-down and select **High**.

   g) On the **Task** tab, select **Recurrence**.

   Recurrence

h) The **Task Recurrence** dialog box appears.

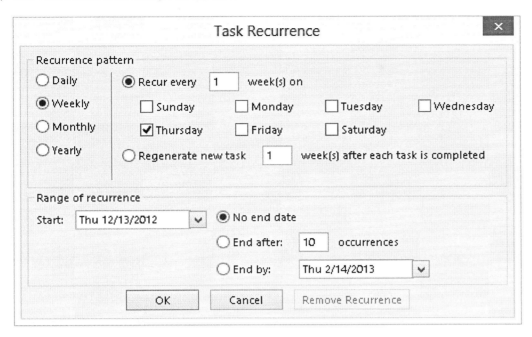

i) In the **Recurrence pattern** section, verify that the task is set to recur weekly, every week on Thursday.

j) In the **Range of recurrence** section, select the **End by** radio button and leave the date as is.

k) In the **Task Recurrence** dialog box, select **OK**.

l) Select **Save & Close** in the **Task** form.

2. View the "Prepare Weekly Meeting Agenda" task in the places it appears in Outlook.

   a) Verify that the "Prepare Weekly Meeting Agenda" task now appears in your list of tasks in the **Content** pane.

   b) Select the **VIEW** tab and, in the **Layout** command group, select **Reading Pane→Right**.

   c) Select the **Prepare Weekly Meeting Agenda** task in the list of your tasks in the **Content** pane (if necessary), and view the details of the task in the **Reading** pane.

   d) Select the **VIEW** tab, and in the **Layout** command group, select **To-Do Bar** and select **Tasks**.

   e) Verify that the **To-Do Bar** appears at the right of the window, and that the task appears in the **Tasks** component of the **To-Do Bar**.

    Note: You may have to expand the **Arrange By** section of the task list in the **To-Do Bar** in order to see your tasks.

   f) Close the **Tasks** component of the **To-Do Bar**.

3. Edit the "Prepare Weekly Meeting Agenda" task to include a reminder and a color category.

   a) In the task list, double-click the **Prepare Weekly Meeting Agenda** task. The task form opens.

   b) In the task form, check the **Reminder** check box.

   c) Leave the reminder date as is and from the time drop-down, select **10:00 a.m.**

   d) On the **Task** tab, in the **Tags** command group, select **Categorize**.

e) From the gallery, select **Recruitment**.

f) Select **Save & Close**.

TOPIC B

Manage Notes

As you start to use Outlook more frequently, you might find you have more emails that need your attention, more meetings to attend, or more tasks to complete. You might find that you need some way to jot down notes about the activities or information that you are handling. In this topic, you will manage your notes in Outlook using notes.

Technology like Outlook is constantly making it easier to communicate. But with more communication, comes more responsibilities. And more information! How will you keep track of all the information that is flying around between your colleagues in emails or meetings? Outlook provides the **Notes** feature, which lets you use electronic sticky notes to keep track of information, ideas, or even meetings notes and store them in one convenient location in Outlook.

Notes

A *note* in Outlook is an electronic version of a sticky note, where you can capture small pieces of information that you need to remember and don't want to lose or forget. The **Notes** workspace in Outlook is where you can create and manage the notes that you take for yourself using the **Notes** feature.

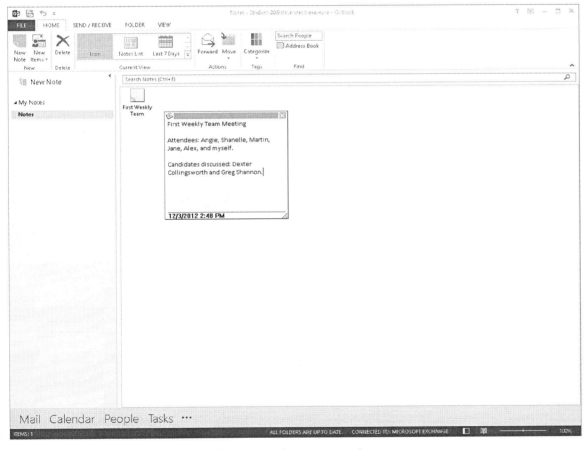

Figure 7-4: An open electronic sticky note in the Notes workspace.

Note: Outlook on the Web

In the online app, you need to access your notes in the **Notes** folder in **Mail**. From within this folder, you can view and delete notes that have been created in the desktop application; however, if you want to create or edit notes, you must do so in the desktop application.

Note Views

You can view the notes you have created in the **Notes** workspace in a variety of ways. These options are found on the **Home** tab on the ribbon, in the **Current View** command group.

- **Icon** displays all of your notes as a sticky note icon. Each icon includes the first line of text in the note as the subject, for context.
- **Notes List** displays all of your notes as a list. Each note in the list includes the first line of the note as a subject, the first three lines of text in the note, the date the note was created, and any categories that have been assigned to the note.
- **Last 7 Days** displays only notes that you created or changed in the last seven days, listed in the **Notes List** view.

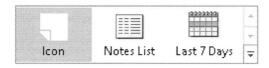

Figure 7-5: Note views.

 Access the Checklist tile on your CHOICE Course screen for reference information and job aids on How to Manage Notes.

ACTIVITY 7-2
Managing Notes

Scenario

Since you will be holding weekly meetings with the recruitment team that is hiring the new employees for Develetech, you want to keep notes of the meetings for yourself. You can use the **Notes** option in Outlook to do so and keep everything in one place.

During your first team meeting, you can take notes for the meeting in Outlook. You want to categorize the note you create and keep it with all the other recruitment items.

After the meeting, you want to print your notes for all of the other meeting participants to have a copy.

---

1. Add the **Notes** launch button to the **Navigation** bar and open the **Notes** workspace.

   a) In the **Navigation** bar, select the **More Options** icon.
   b) Select **Navigation Options**.
   c) In the **Navigation Options** dialog box, using the spin wheel, set the **Maximum number if visible items** field to **5**.
   d) Select **OK**.
   e) Verify that **Notes** is added to the **Navigation** bar.

   Mail Calendar People Tasks Notes •••

   f) Select **Notes**.

2. Create a note for your first weekly team meeting.
   a) On the **HOME** tab, in the **New** command group, select **New Note**.

   New
   Note

   b) In the sticky note with that appears, type *First Weekly Team Meeting*
   c) Press **Enter** twice.
   d) Type *Attendees: Angie, Shanelle, Martin, Jane, Alex, and myself*
   e) Press **Enter** twice.
   f) Type *Candidates discussed: Dexter Collingsworth and Greg Shannon*
   g) Place your cursor over the resizing handle at the bottom right of the sticky note, and drag the corner until the note is large enough to display all your text.
   h) Close the note.

    Note: Your text is automatically saved in the note when you close it.

3. In the **Current View** command group, select **Notes List** to display your notes in a list.

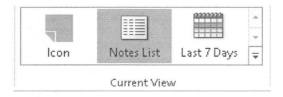

4. Categorize the note with the **Recruitment** color category.
   a) Make sure the that **First Weekly Team Meeting** note is selected.
   b) In the **Tags** command group, select **Categorize** and select the **Recruitment** category.

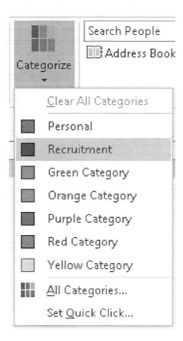

5. Print the "First Weekly Team Meeting" note.
   a) On the ribbon, select **FILE→Print**.
   b) In the **Settings** section, make sure that the default **Memo Style** option is selected.
   c) View how your note will look in the preview pane.
   d) Select **Print**.

Summary

In this lesson, you used the **Tasks** and **Notes** features in Outlook to help you manage the more personal items you have to handle on a daily basis. Using tasks can help you keep track of any activities that you are responsible for completing in a timely manner, and notes can help you keep track of information or details that you may need to remember. And, Outlook lets you store these personal items alongside the mail, calendar, and contact items you already work with on a daily basis in Outlook, allowing you to keep track of everything all in one location.

Do you think you will use the Tasks feature? If so, how?

Do you think you will use the Notes feature? If so, how?

 Note: Check your CHOICE Course screen for opportunities to interact with your classmates, peers, and the larger CHOICE online community about the topics covered in this course or other topics you are interested in. From the Course screen you can also access available resources for a more continuous learning experience.

8 | Customizing the Outlook Environment

Lesson Time: 25 minutes

Lesson Objectives

In this lesson, you will:

- Customize the Outlook interface.

- Create and manage Quick Steps.

Lesson Introduction

You are now familiar with all of the major workspaces in Microsoft® Office Outlook®. You can manage messages in your **Mail** workspace; manage your calendar entries in the **Calendar** workspace; manage your contacts in the **Contacts** workspace; and use **Tasks** and **Notes** to manage your more individualized items. Now, you want to be able to personalize and customize the interface to suit your own personal needs and preferences. In this lesson, you will customize the Outlook environment.

An application like Outlook comes with a lot of standard settings and default configurations. For many people, the way that Outlook looks and behaves out of the box will be good enough for them. However, many people may find that these defaults do not suit their personal needs or preferences, that the way things look or work do not allow them to be most efficient when performing functions in Outlook. Fortunately, you can customize many configurations in Outlook to help you best utilize the many components of the Outlook environment.

TOPIC A

Customize the Outlook Interface

Now that you know how to perform all of the basic functions of all the available tools and workspaces in Outlook, you might find the default configurations do not suit your own personal preferences or needs. Outlook provides a number of ways in which you can customize your interface to look and behave in ways that are convenient to your personal use. In this topic, you will customize the Outlook interface.

Outlook Interface Options

You can use the customizations that are available in Outlook to define the look and feel of Outlook to serve your own personal preferences and needs. You can add and remove commands on the ribbon and the Quick Access Toolbar. You can also change default settings for the **Mail**, **Calendar**, **People**, and **Tasks** workspaces which gives you control over the behavior and appearance of selected features. For example, you can choose how you want to be notified when a new message arrives—with an audio alert or a visual alert displayed on screen or both.

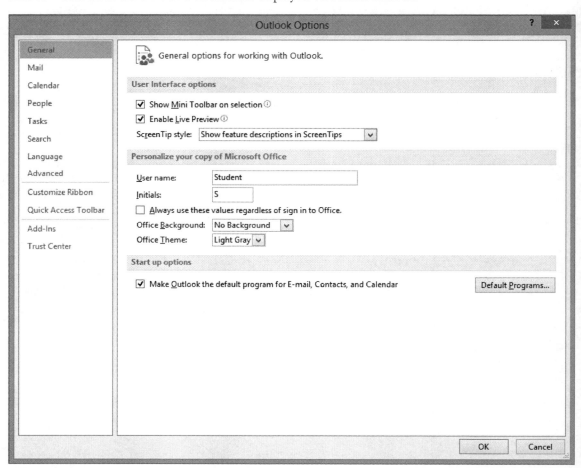

Figure 8-1: Outlook Options dialog box.

In the **Outlook Options** dialog box, settings are grouped into categories that appear in the left pane. After modifying the desired settings, be sure to save your changes by selecting **OK** in the lower-right corner of the dialog box.

Note: Outlook on the Web

You can change the default settings of the online app environment to suit your working style. By selecting the **Settings** icon at the right end of the Office 365 header, you have access to a variety of Outlook options, such as creating an email signature and controlling new message notifications. The next course, *Microsoft® Office Outlook® 2013: Part 2,* will address many of the features that are controlled in the online **Settings** pane.

Access the Checklist tile on your CHOICE Course screen for reference information and job aids on How to Customize the Appearance of the Outlook Interface.

ACTIVITY 8-1
Customizing the Outlook Interface

Scenario

There are many components of Outlook that display by default or are displayed with default configurations upon installation. Since you will be using Outlook on a daily basis at Develetech as your organization's email client, you want to customize the interface to suit your needs and personal preferences.

1. In the **Navigation** bar, select **Mail** to return to the **Mail** workspace.

2. Change the background and theme of the Outlook interface.

   a) On the ribbon, select **FILE→Options**. The **Outlook Options** dialog box opens, with the **General** tab displayed.
   b) In the **Personalize your copy of Microsoft Office** section, select **Office Background** and view the background options available.
   c) From the drop-down, select a background of your choice.
   d) From the **Office Theme** drop-down, select **Dark Gray**.
   e) Select **OK** in the **Outlook Options** dialog box.
   f) View how your selected changes look in the Outlook interface.

3. Customize the ribbon for the **Mail** workspace by adding a new tab and command group that houses the **Empty Deleted Items** command.

   a) Select **FILE→Options** to open the **Outlook Options** dialog box.
   b) Select the **Customize Ribbon** tab.
   c) At the right, in the **Customize the Ribbon** section, select **New Tab**.

d) Verify that **New Tab (Custom)** including **New Group (Custom)** was created and added after the **Home (Mail)** tab in the **Main Tabs** list.

```
Main Tabs
☐ ✔ Home (Mail)
☐ ✔ Home (Calendar Table View)
☐ ✔ Home (Calendar)
☐ ✔ Home (Contacts)
☐ ✔ Home (Tasks)
☐ ✔ Home (Notes)
    ☐ New
    ☐ Delete
    ☐ Current View
    ☐ Actions
    ☐ Tags
    ☐ Find
☐ ✔ New Tab (Custom)
        New Group (Custom)
☐ ✔ Home (Journals)
☐ ✔ Send / Receive
☐ ✔ Folder
☐ ✔ View
☐ ☐ Developer
☐ ✔ Add-Ins
```

e) In the **Main Tabs** list, select **New Tab (Custom)**.

f) Select **Rename**.

g) In the **Rename** dialog box, in the **Display name** field, type *My New Tab* and select **OK**.

h) Rename **New Group** to *My New Group* and select **OK**.

i) Verify that **My New Group** is selected in the **Main Tabs** list.

j) In the **Choose commands from** drop-down in the left pane, select **All Commands** .

k) In the list, find and select **Empty Deleted Items**

l) Select **Add**

m) Verify that the **Empty Deleted Items** command now appears below **My New Group** in the **Main Tabs** list.

n) Select **OK** in the **Outlook Options** dialog box.

o) Verify that the **My New Tab** tab appears on the ribbon, to the right of the **HOME** tab.

p) Select **My New Tab** and verify that the **My New Group** command group and the **Empty Deleted Items** command appear.

4. Customize the **Quick Access Toolbar** to include the **Print** and **Save As** commands..

a) Select **FILE→Options**.

b) Select **Quick Access Toolbar**.

c) In the **Choose commands from** list, select **Print**.

d) Select **Add** and verify that the **Print** command now appears in the **Customize Quick Access Toolbar** list.

e) Add the **Save As** command in the same manner.

f) Select **OK** in the **Outlook Options** dialog box.

g) Verify that the **Print** and **Save As** commands now display in the **Quick Access Toolbar** at the top left of the Outlook window.

Note: Customized views only apply to the current folder and workspace in which you are working, but you can apply them to other folders. For more information about how to apply your customized view to other locations, check out the LearnTO **Apply Your Customized View to Other Folders In Outlook** presentation from the **LearnTO** tile on the CHOICE Course screen.

TOPIC B

Create and Manage Quick Steps

Now that you have customized the way that Outlook looks and feels, you might consider customizing more complex ways that Outlook acts. Outlook comes with preconfigured Quick Steps that you can use to perform commonly used actions or commands, and you can customize or create new Quick Steps to suit your own needs. In this topic, you will create and manage Quick Steps.

Outlook comes out of the box with a number of Quick Steps preconfigured. These Quick Steps are assumptions: they assume that these are the functions or actions that you might perform most often. What if the preconfigured Quick Steps don't meet your needs? You can create or manage the Quick Steps to better suit the ways in which you are using Outlook and the actions you are taking most often.

Quick Steps

Quick Steps take common tasks that usually require multiple actions to perform and simplify them into a one-step command. The Quick Step commands are found on the **HOME** tab in the **Mail** workspace, in the **Quick Steps** command group. Outlook comes with a number of default Quick Steps, and you can customize or create new Quick Steps to suit your needs.

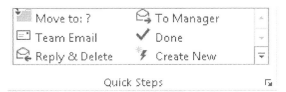

Figure 8-2: Quick Steps are displayed on the HOME tab in the Mail workspace.

The default Quick Steps provided in Outlook include:

- **Move To** marks a selected email message as read and moves it to a specified folder, which you choose the first time the Quick Step is used.
- **Team Email** forwards a selected email message to the members of your team, which you choose the first time the Quick Step is used.
- **Reply & Delete** replies to a selected email message and deletes the original message and moves it to the **Deleted Items** folder.
- **To Manager** forwards a selected email message to your manager, which you choose the first time the Quick Step is used.
- **Done** marks a selected email message as read or complete and moves it to a specified folder, which you choose the first time the Quick Step is used.
- **Create New** opens the **Edit Quick Step** dialog box, where you can create a new Quick Step.

> **Note: Outlook on the Web**
>
> This feature is not available in the online app. If you want to use Quick Steps to manage your email, then you must use the desktop application.

The Manage Quick Steps Dialog Box

You can use the **Manage Quick Steps** dialog box to create new Quick Steps and manage your existing Quick Steps. To open the **Manage Quick Steps** dialog box, select the dialog box launcher in the **Quick Steps** command group.

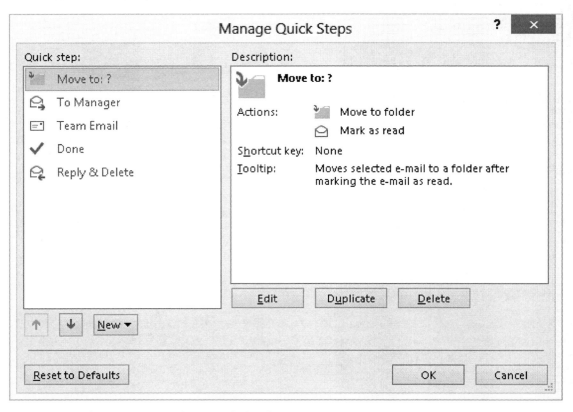

Figure 8–3: The Manage Quick Steps dialog box.

There are several components of the **Manage Quick Steps** dialog box that you should be familiar with to help you manage your Quick Steps.

Component	Description
Quick step list	Displays the list of Quick Steps that currently appear in your **Quick Steps** command group. Includes default Quick Steps and any custom Quick Steps you have created.
Description pane	Displays the description of a Quick Step that you have selected in the **Quick Step** list. The description includes the actions associated with the Quick Step, if a shortcut key has been set for the Quick Step, and a Tooltip description for the Quick Step.
Edit	Opens the **Edit Quick Step** dialog box, where you can edit the selected Quick Step and the actions the command performs.
Duplicate	Creates a copy of the selected Quick Step and opens the **Edit Quick Step** dialog box. You can give a name to the Quick Step, make any changes to the actions that the command performs, and save the duplicate as a new Quick Step.
Delete	Deletes the selected Quick Step, and removes it from both the **Quick Step** list and the **Quick Steps** command group.
Up and **Down** arrows	Allows you to rearrange the order in which the Quick Steps appear in both the **Quick Step** list and in the **Quick Steps** command group.

Component	Description
New	Displays the options available for creating a new Quick Step, which include **Move to Folder, Categorize and Move, Flag and Move, New e-mail to, Forward to, New Meeting with,** and **Custom**. If you choose **Custom,** the **Edit Quick Step** dialog box opens, where you can create your own customized Quick Step from scratch.
Reset to Defaults	Resets all of the Quick Steps to default settings.

 Access the Checklist tile on your CHOICE Course screen for reference information and job aids on How to Manage Quick Steps.

ACTIVITY 8–2
Creating and Managing Quick Steps

Scenario

Outlook comes with a number of preconfigured Quick Steps. You don't necessarily need to use all of the Quick Steps provided, but you think you could use Quick Steps to your advantage. You want to manage the Quick Steps to remove some of the preconfigured Quick Steps and add a new Quick Step to perform an action you do often: create a task from a message.

1. Remove the **To Manager** and **Team Email** Quick Steps.
    a) On the **HOME** tab, in the **Quick Steps** command group, select the dialog box launcher to open the **Manage Quick Steps** dialog box.

    b) In the **Quick Step** section, select the **To Manager** Quick Step and select **Delete**.
    c) Verify that the **Team Email** Quick Step is selected automatically, and select **Delete**.

2. Create a new Quick Step to create a task from a message.

a) In the **Manage Quick Steps** dialog box, select **New** and select **Custom**.

b) In the **Edit Quick Step** dialog box, in the **Name** field, type *Create Task From Message*
c) From the **Choose an Action** drop-down, find and select **Create a task with text of message**.
d) In the **Edit Quick Step** dialog box, select **Finish**.
e) Verify that the **Create Task From Message** appears in the **Quick Step** list in the **Manage Quick Steps** dialog box.
f) Select **OK** in the **Manage Quick Steps** dialog box.
g) Verify that the **Quick Steps** command group displays the new Quick Step.

3. Perform the **Create Task From Message** Quick Step.
    a) In the message list, find and select the email from David McMurtry with the subject line "New Travel Company and Contact."
    b) In the **Quick Steps** command group, select **Create Task From Message**.
    c) A new task form will open with the subject "New Travel Company and Contact."
    d) In the **Subject** field, delete the text and type *Contact New Travel Rep*
    e) In the **Start date** field, select the calendar icon ⊞ and from the calendar, select the following day's date.
    f) Verify that the **Due date** field automatically populates with the date.
    g) In the task body, select the blank space above the dashed line and type *Contact the new travel rep to make travel arrangements for the convention next month.*
    h) Select **Save & Close**.

Summary

In this lesson, you customized the Outlook environment. The default configurations in Outlook may not meet your personal needs or preferences, and may actually make working in Outlook harder for you. Knowing how to customize the way that Outlook appears and behaves can help you to work more efficiently in the environment.

Will you use the default configurations in Outlook, or will you customize your environment? Why or why not?

Are Quick Steps a feature of Outlook that you envision using? How might they be useful to you?

 Note: Check your CHOICE Course screen for opportunities to interact with your classmates, peers, and the larger CHOICE online community about the topics covered in this course or other topics you are interested in. From the Course screen you can also access available resources for a more continuous learning experience.

Course Follow-Up

Congratulations! You have completed the *Microsoft® Office Outlook® 2013: Part 1* course. You have successfully used Outlook to manage the numerous aspects of communicating electronically, including managing email communications, managing calendar events, managing your contacts, and using other features like tasks and notes to communicate with yourself.

The need to share important information quickly and easily has greatly affected the ways in which we communicate. And as the technology has evolved to meet those needs, communication via email and other electronic forms has grown exponentially. As the use of email has grown in popularity as *the* method of communication, especially in the business sector, most organizations have found the need to implement a corporate mail management system such as Microsoft Outlook to handle the emails and meeting invitations sent between employees. Knowing how to use all of the basic functions Outlook provides to simplify and unify corporate communications—email, calendar invites, and contacts—will allow you to communicate with others more quickly and easily.

What's Next?

Microsoft® Office Outlook® 2013: Part 2 is the next course in this series. Part 2 of the series focuses on using the features of Outlook you learned about in Part 1, but in a more advanced manner. You will learn about advanced message options and message management, advanced contact and calendar management, and using more advanced features of Outlook like the journal, sharing folders, and managing Outlook data files.

Microsoft® 365™: Web Apps (with Skype® for Business) provides an introduction to using Office in a cloud-based environment. In this course, you will use Microsoft® Outlook® mail, Skype for Business instant messaging and online meetings, and Microsoft® SharePoint® Team Sites to work and collaborate on Office Online documents.

You are encouraged to explore Outlook further by actively participating in any of the social media forums set up by your instructor or training administrator through the **Social Media** tile on the CHOICE Course screen.

A | Microsoft Office Outlook 2013 Exam 77-423

Selected Logical Operations courseware addresses Microsoft Office Specialist (MOS) certification skills for Microsoft Office 2013. The following table indicates where Outlook 2013 skills that are tested on Exam 77-423 are covered in the Logical Operations Outlook 2013 series of courses.

Objective Domain	Covered In
1.0 Manage the Outlook Environment	
1.1 Customize Outlook Settings	
1.1.1 Include original messages with all reply messages	Part 1, Topic 3-C
1.1.2 Change text formats for all outgoing messages	Part 1, Topic 2-C
1.1.3 Customize the Navigation Pane	Part 1, Topic 8-A
1.1.4 Block specific addresses	Part 2
1.1.5 Configure views	Part 1, Topics 3-A, 5-A, 6-B, 7-A, 7-B
1.1.6 Manage multiple accounts	Part 2
1.1.7 Set Outlook options	Part 2
1.2 Automate Outlook	
1.2.1 Change quoted text colors	Part 1, Topic 2-F
1.2.2 Create and assign signatures	Part 1, Topic 2-F
1.2.3 Apply Quick Steps	Part 1, Topic 8-B
1.2.4 Create and manage rules	Part 2
1.2.5 Create auto-replies	Part 2
1.3 Print and Save Information in Outlook	
1.3.1 Print messages	Part 1, Topic 1-B
1.3.2 Print calendars	Part 1, Topic 5-D
1.3.3 Save message attachments	Part 1, Topic 3-B
1.3.4 Preview attachments	Part 1, Topic 3-B
1.3.5 Print contacts	Part 1, Topic 6-B
1.3.6 Print tasks	Part 1, Topic 7-A
1.3.7 Save messages in alternate formats	Part 2

Objective Domain	Covered In
1.3.8 Create data files	Part 2
1.4. Search in Outlook	
1.4.1 Create new search folders	Part 2
1.4.2 Search for messages	Part 2
1.4.3 Search for tasks	Part 2
1.4.4 Search for contacts	Part 2
1.4.5 Search calendars	Part 2
1.4.6 Use Advanced Find	Part 2
1.4.7 Use Search by Location	Part 2
2.0 Manage Messages	
2.1 Create a Message	
2.1.1 Create messages	Part 1, Topics 1-B, 2-A
2.1.2 Forward messages	Part 1, Topic 1-B
2.1.3 Delete messages	Part 1, Topic 1-B
2.1.4 Add/remove message attachments	Part 1, Topics 2-D, 3-C
2.1.5 Add Cc and Bcc to messages	Part 1, Topics 1-B, 2-A
2.1.6 Add voting options to messages	Part 1, Topic 3-C
2.1.7 Reply to all	Part 1, Topic 1-B
2.1.8 Reply to sender only	Part 1, Topic 1-B
2.1.9 Prioritize messages	Part 1, Topic 3-C
2.1.10 Mark as private	Part 2
2.1.11 Request delivery/read receipt	Part 1, Topic 3-C
2.1.12 Redirect replies	Part 2
2.1.13 Delegate access	Part 2
2.2 Format a Message	
2.2.1 Format text	Part 1, Topic 2-C
2.2.2 Insert hyperlinks	Part 2
2.2.3 Apply themes and styles	Part 1, Topic 2-E
2.2.4 Insert images	Part 1, Topic 2-E
2.2.5 Add a signature to specific messages	Part 1, Topic 2-F
2.2.6 Format signatures	Part 1, Topic 2-F
2.2.7 Create and use Quick Parts	Part 2
2.3 Organize and Manage Messages	
2.3.1 Sort messages	Part 2
2.3.2 Move messages between folders	Part 1, Topic 4-B
2.3.3 Add new local folders	Part 1, Topic 4-B

Objective Domain	Covered In
2.3.4 Apply categories	Part 1, Topic 4-A
2.3.5 Configure junk email settings	Part 2
2.3.6 Cleanup messages	Part 1, Topic 4-A
2.3.7 Mark as read/unread	Part 1, Topic 4-A
2.3.8 Flag messages	Part 1, Topic 4-A
2.3.9 Ignore messages	Part 1, Topic 4-A
2.3.10 Sort by conversation	Part 1, Topic 3-A
2.3.11 Set attachment reminder options	Part 1, Topic 2-D
3.0 Manage Schedules	
3.1 Create and Manage Calendars	
3.1.1 Adjust viewing details for calendars	Part 1, Topic 5-A
3.1.2 Modify calendar time zones	Part 2
3.1.3 Delete calendars	Part 2
3.1.4 Demonstrate how to set calendar work times	Part 2
3.1.5 Create multiple calendars	Part 2
3.1.6 Manage calendar groups	Part 2
3.1.7 Overlay calendars	Part 2
3.1.8 Share calendars	Part 2
3.2 Create Appointments, Meetings, and Events	
3.2.1 Create calendar item	Part 1, Topics 5-A, 5-B
3.2.2 Create recurring calendar items	Part 1, Topics 5-A, 5-B
3.2.3 Cancel calendar items	Part 1, Topic 5-B
3.2.4 Create calendar items from messages	Part 1, Topics 5-A, 5-B
3.2.5 Set calendar item times	Part 1, Topics 5-A, 5-B
3.2.6 Categorize calendar items	Part 1, Topics 5-A, 5-B
3.2.7 Use the Scheduling Assistant	Part 1, Topic 5-B
3.2.8 Change availability status	Part 1, Topic 5-B
3.2.9 Schedule resources	Part 1, Topic 5-B
3.2.10 Utilize Room Finder	Part 1, Topic 5-B
3.3 Organize and Manage Appointments, Meetings, and Events	
3.3.1 Set calendar item importance	Part 1, Topics 5-A, 5-B
3.3.2 Forward calendar items	Part 1, Topics 5-A, 5-B
3.3.3 Configure reminders	Part 1, Topics 5-A, 5-B, Part 2
3.3.4 Add participants	Part 1, Topic 5-B
3.3.5 Respond to invitations	Part 1, Topic 5-B

Objective Domain	Covered In
3.3.6 Update calendar items	Part 1, Topics 5-A, 5-B
3.3.7 Share meeting notes	Part 1, Topic 5-B
3.4 Create and Manage Notes, Tasks, and Journals	
3.4.1 Create and manage tasks	Part 1, Topic 7-A, Part 2
3.4.2 Create and manage notes	Part 1, Topic 7-B
3.4.3 Attach notes to contacts	Part 1, Topic 6-A
3.4.4 Create journal entries	Part 2
3.4.5 Update task status	Part 1, Topic 7-B, Part 2
4.0 Manage Contacts and Groups	
4.1 Create and Manage Contacts	
4.1.1 Create new contacts	Part 1, Topic 6-A
4.1.2 Delete contacts	Part 1, Topic 6-A
4.1.3 Import contacts from external sources	Part 1, Topic 6-A
4.1.4 Edit contact information	Part 1, Topic 6-A
4.1.5 Attach an image to contacts	Part 1, Topic 6-A
4.1.6 Add tags to contacts	Part 1, Topic 6-B
4.1.7 Share contacts	Part 2
4.1.8 Manage multiple address books	Part 1, Topic 6-A
4.2 Create and Manage Groups	
4.2.1 Create new contact groups	Part 2
4.2.2 Add contacts to existing groups	Part 2
4.2.3 Add notes to a group	Part 2
4.2.4 Update contacts within groups	Part 2
4.2.5 Delete groups	Part 2
4.2.6 Delete group members	Part 2

B | Microsoft Outlook 2013 Common Keyboard Shortcuts

The following table lists common keyboard shortcuts you can use in Outlook 2013.

Function	Shortcut
Go to the **Search** box	**F3** or **Ctrl+E**
Use **Advanced Find**	**Ctrl+Shift+F**
Create an appointment (when in Calendar)	**Ctrl+N**
Create a contact (when in Contacts)	**Ctrl+N**
Create a message (when in Mail)	**Ctrl+N**
Create a task (when in Tasks)	**Ctrl+N**
Undo	**Ctrl+Z** or **Alt+Backspace**
Delete an item	**Ctrl+D**
Print	**Ctrl+P**
Check spelling	**F7**
Forward a message	**Ctrl+F**
Reply to a message	**Ctrl+R**
Reply all to a message	**Ctrl+Shift+R**
Open the Address Book	**Ctrl+Shift+B**
Find a contact	**F11**
Accept a task request	**Alt+C**
Decline a task request	**Alt+D**
Display the **Format** menu	**Alt+O**
Display the **Font** dialog box	**Ctrl+Shift+P**
Insert a hyperlink	**Ctrl+K**

Lesson Labs

Lesson labs are provided for certain lessons as additional learning resources for this course. Lesson labs are developed for selected lessons within a course in cases when they seem most instructionally useful as well as technically feasible. In general, labs are supplemental, optional unguided practice and may or may not be performed as part of the classroom activities. Your instructor will consider setup requirements, classroom timing, and instructional needs to determine which labs are appropriate for you to perform, and at what point during the class. If you do not perform the labs in class, your instructor can tell you if you can perform them independently as self-study, and if there are any special setup requirements.

Lesson Lab 2–1
Composing an Email

Activity Time: 10 minutes

Data Files

C:\091043Data\Composing Messages\Amy Reynolds Resume.docx

C:\091043Data\Composing Messages\Amy Reynolds Sample.png

C:\091043Data\Composing Messages\Interview Schedule.docx

Scenario

You want to send an email to the recruitment team with some information about another of the prospective candidates for the multimedia position, Amy Reynolds. In this practice lab, you will compose, spell check, and format the email, and then attach Amy's résumé, insert a sample of her work, and use the screenshot tool to take and insert a screenshot of the interview schedule in your email.

---

1. Open a new message form.

2. Select the recruitment team members as recipients of the email.

3. Compose your message.

4. Check spelling and grammar in the email message.

5. Format your message text to suit your preferences.

6. Attach Amy Reynolds' résumé to the email for your colleagues to review.

7. Insert the sample of Amy's work into the email message.

8. Use the screenshot tool to take a screenshot of the interview schedule and insert it in the email message.

9. Send the message.

Lesson Lab 3-1
Enabling Message Preview and Conversations

Activity Time: 10 minutes

Scenario

You want to customize your reading options to be able to read and respond to your Outlook items more quickly and easily. In this practice lab, you will enable Message Preview and conversations for your email messages.

 Note: Please note, should you choose to do this lab, you will want to disable both AutoPreview and conversations once you have completed this activity. Leaving Message Preview and conversations enabled may affect the way that other activities work in this course.

1. Modify the Message Preview options for items in your message list.

2. Show messages in the Inbox as conversations.

3. Configure how messages and message threads are displayed in a conversation.

4. Explore how Message Preview and conversations look in the Inbox.

5. Modify Message Preview to the default configuration and disable conversations for your folders.

Lesson Lab 4–1
Exploring Ways to Manage Messages

Activity Time: 10 minutes

Scenario

You can use the many options available in Outlook to help you manage and organize your messages. In this practice lab, you will explore using tags, flags, commands, and folders to manage your messages.

1. Create a new color category and categorize messages or items in your inbox using the new category.

2. Flag messages or items in your message list for follow-up.

3. Use the **Clean Up** command to remove redundant emails from a folder.

4. Create a new folder and move some of your message or items from your Inbox into the new folder.

Lesson Lab 5–1
Managing Recurring Calendar Entries

Activity Time: 10 minutes

Scenario

You take a kickboxing class every Wednesday from 5:30 p.m to 7 p.m. at Bit by Bit Fitness. You want to add the class as a recurring appointment on your calendar.

You created a recurring weekly meeting with the recruitment team, but you forgot to include one of the team members, Martin Smith, on the meeting request. You need to send an update for the Weekly Recruitment Team Meeting to include Martin Smith as an attendee.

1. Create an appointment for the kickboxing class.

2. Display the time on your calendar as **Out of Office**.

3. Create a reminder for the appointment.

4. Make the appointment recurring, with 10 recurrences.

5. Categorize the appointment with the **Personal** color category.

6. Schedule the recurring appointment.

7. Verify that the kickboxing appointment appears on the following week as well, to verify that the appointment was scheduled as recurring appropriately.

8. Update the Weekly Recruitment Team Meeting in your calendar to include Martin Smith as a required attendee, and send the update only to Martin.

Lesson Lab 6-1

Creating a Secondary Address Book and Importing Contacts

Activity Time: 10 minutes

Data File

C:\091043Data\Managing Your Contacts\Personal Contacts.csv

Scenario

You can use the Global Address List for Develetech in Outlook or the list of contacts you have created to send emails to those people you communicate with on a professional level. Sometimes, you may use your work email address to send emails to your personal contacts. You want to keep your personal contacts separate from your professional contacts, so you will create a secondary address book for them.

You have saved an Excel file of the contact information for some personal contacts from another email account and email client that you use for more personal communications. Once you have created the secondary address book to contain them, you can import these personal contacts.

1. Create a secondary address book called *My Personal Contacts*

2. Import your personal contacts in the **Personal Contacts** Excel file to the **My Personal Contacts** folder.

3. Verify that a contact for each personal contact you imported now appears in the contact list in **My Personal Contacts**.

Lesson Lab 7–1
Forwarding a Note

Activity Time: 10 minutes

Scenario

Recently, you used the **Notes** feature to take notes about what was discussed during your weekly meeting with the recruitment team. You want to forward those notes to all the members of the recruitment team.

1. Find and select the **First Weekly Team Meeting** note in your **Notes** list.

2. Forward the note to Alex Jaffey, Jane Woodward, and Martin Smith.

Glossary

address book
A repository where your contacts are stored.

appointment
An activity that you can schedule in your calendar and does not require inviting other people or using other resources such as an online meeting or conference room. Appointments are created and managed using the Calendar workspace in Outlook.

attachment
A document or file that is included and sent along with your email message.

attachment preview
A feature in Outlook that allows you to preview a file that has been attached to an email message in the **Reading** pane.

AutoCorrect
A tool that checks for common typing errors, including spelling and grammar errors, capitalization mistakes, and other typographical mistakes. If it can determine what was intended, it will automatically correct the error; if not, it will offer suggestions for how to fix the error.

AutoCorrect Tool
A tool in Outlook that checks for common typing errors, including spelling and grammar errors, capitalization mistakes, and other typographical mistakes.

color categories
Color codes that you can customize and assign to items to help you visually organize and keep track of your items.

contact
Any person with whom you need to communicate with for business or personal reasons.

conversations
An organizational tool in Outlook where all messages that you have sent or received and which have the same subject line are grouped together with the subject line as the heading.

desktop alerts
Notifications that appear on screen when a new Outlook item, such as an email message or meeting invitation, is delivered and arrives in your inbox.

Dialog Box Launchers
A small downward-arrow button located at the bottom-right corner of the command group box which, when selected, opens a dialog box with additional features available for that command group.

event
An appointment or meeting that is intended to last all day.

folders
The organizational containers in which items in Outlook are stored.

gallery
A library of all the options that are available for a specific command.

Global Address List
A list of all users, shared resources, and distribution groups that have been created and networked on the Microsoft Exchange Server for an organization.

items
Contain the information that you are viewing or working with. Items in Outlook include email messages, calendar entries, contact information, tasks, and notes.

Live Preview
A feature in Outlook and other Office products that provides you with a "sneak peek" of what your formatting changes will look like if they were applied before actually applying those changes.

MailTips
A feature that provides real-time feedback to you concerning the messages you are composing, as they are being composed and displays text about the issue in the item form to notify you of the potential problem. This feature is only available when Outlook is configured with a Microsoft Exchange Server.

meeting
An activity that you can schedule on your calendar and requires inviting other people and possibly requires utilizing other resources available in Outlook. Meetings are created and managed using the Calendar workspace in Outlook.

Message Preview
A feature in Outlook that displays the first few lines of a message in the Content pane, beneath the subject line of the message.

Microsoft Exchange Server
A mail server application that acts as the communication platform that manages and filters email messages and other types of communications, such as meeting invitations, that are sent over a network.

Mini Toolbar
A floating toolbar that appears when text has been selected in the body of your Outlook message, and provides access to the formatting tools, without having to access these tools from the ribbon.

notes
An electronic version of a sticky note, where you can capture small pieces of information that you need to remember and don't want to lose or forget. Notes are created and managed using the Notes workspace in Outlook.

People Hub
The new default view for contacts in Outlook 2013. In the People Hub, all of the contacts that have saved or added appear, even contacts added from social networks.

personal folders
Folders you can create in Outlook that are saved as personal store table (.pst) files and are stored on the local computer, rather than the Exchange server.

Quick Steps
Commands in Outlook which take common tasks that usually require multiple actions to perform and simplify them into a one-step command.

secondary address books
Additional address books that you can create in Outlook, name at your discretion, and use to store your contacts. Contacts are created and managed using the Contacts workspace in Outlook.

signature
A standard closing element that can be created, personalized, and then added to the end of your email messages.

SmartArt
A tool in Outlook and other Office suite products that allows you to organize your information into a graphical layout to more effectively communicate your ideas or convey your messages.

styles

Preconfigured formatting options that can be applied to messages or other Outlook items such as font type, font color, paragraph spacing, and bulleted lists, and can be edited to suit individual needs.

task

An action item, activity, or piece of work that is assigned to you and that must be completed within a certain time frame. Tasks are created and managed using the Tasks workspace in Outlook.

themes

Preconfigured design and formatting options that can be applied to your message to ensure consistency in all content that you create or place in the message body.

Index

V

views
    pane *87*
voting options
    in email *96*

W

WordArt *67*
workspaces
    Calendar *12*
    Contacts *13*
    Journal *14*
    Mail *8*
    Notes *14, 187*
    Tasks *14, 182*